IMAGES
*of America*

# JEWISH
# GOLD COUNTRY

**ON THE COVER:** High in the mountains of Placer County, the Gold Rush town of Last Chance got its name from adventurous miners. Before declining into a ghost town, Last Chance boasted several saloons and businesses, two fraternal lodges, and a number of permanent residents. Blue Eyes Mine, shown here in 1882, was one of the area's attractions. (Courtesy of Western States Jewish History Association Archives.)

IMAGES
*of America*

# JEWISH
# GOLD COUNTRY

Jonathan L. Friedmann

ARCADIA
PUBLISHING

Published by Arcadia Publishing
Charleston, South Carolina

Printed in the United States of America

Library of Congress Control Number: 2019951198

For all general information, please contact Arcadia Publishing:
Telephone 843-853-2070
Fax 843-853-0044
E-mail sales@arcadiapublishing.com
For customer service and orders:
Toll-Free 1-888-313-2665

Visit us on the Internet at www.arcadiapublishing.com

# CONTENTS

# ACKNOWLEDGMENTS

This book is indebted to the painstaking work of Dr. Norton Stern (1920–1992), a California-based optometrist, Hebrew school principal, and founding editor of the quarterly journal *Western States Jewish History* (est. 1968), and his longtime collaborator William M. Kramer (1920–2004), a Los Angeles rabbi, lawyer, and professor. Over several decades, these pioneer researchers collected thousands of documents chronicling the early Jewish experience in the American West: photographs, advertisements, newspaper articles, government records, family histories, political membership lists, receipts, letters, diaries, interviews, posters, business cards, and more. Rabbi Kramer maintained the archives and published the journal after Stern's death in 1992. David W. Epstein (publisher and managing editor) and Gladys Sturman (publisher and editor-in-chief) took over the journal and archives in 1998. After their retirement in late 2018, David asked me to succeed him as president of the Western States Jewish History Association and director of the Jewish Museum of the American West, an online museum of over 600 exhibits. I am grateful to David for giving me this unique opportunity, and to John F. Guest, who joined me as the association's vice president. Thank you to Erin L. Vosgien, acquisitions editor at Arcadia Publishing, who invited me to put this book together, and to Caroline Anderson, title manager at Arcadia, who took it from there. Lastly, I am thankful for my wife, Elvia, whose patience, encouragement, and support are behind everything I do.

All images in this book are from the Western States Jewish History Association Archives.

# INTRODUCTION

The discovery of gold on January 24, 1848, in Coloma, north-central California, initiated a gold rush that would bring hundreds of thousands to the foothills of the Sierra Nevada. An international cast of gold-seekers, merchants, and tradespeople arrived via overland trails and through the port of San Francisco. By 1852, San Francisco had grown from a small settlement of about 200 residents to a boomtown of 36,000. Almost overnight, towns and mining camps sprang up along the Mother Lode, an alignment of hard-rock gold deposits stretching from the northwest to the southeast in the Sierra Nevada. Adjacent areas developed farms, ranches, and shops to meet the needs of miners and settlers. Solitary prospectors with pickaxes and pans were soon replaced by sophisticated mining companies, which introduced flumes, hydraulic systems, and newfangled machinery. Shops and living quarters evolved from canvas tents to wooden structures to fireproof brick buildings, signaling that the new arrivals were there to stay.

Gold Rush prosperity was not shared equally. Most of the easily mined areas were quickly claimed and exhausted. White settlers soon realized that luck and timing, not hard work or persistence, determined who struck it rich. With support from California's state government, established on September 9, 1850, whites lashed out at non-whites who competed for scarce mining spots and even scarcer gold. Miners from Mexico, Latin America, and China suffocated under heavy taxes, and violent incidents were commonplace. Indigenous peoples suffered genocide at the hands of state militias, federal troops, volunteer military companies, and vigilantes. Already depleted from 300,000 in 1769, when the first California mission was built, to 150,000 in the 1840s, there were just 30,000 California Indians left by the 1860s.

By and large, Jews drawn to Northern California from Europe and the Eastern United States escaped racially driven attacks. Anti-Semitism was rare in California during the 19th and early 20th centuries. The Jews' European skin tone allowed them to "pass" as whites, and their general avoidance of mining kept them away from bloody turf wars. Jewish settlers, many of whom had backgrounds as merchants and peddlers, opened stores and businesses in small towns and mining camps. Although they came from different regions, spoke different languages, and had different customs, they all embraced the ethos of the self-made "Western man," believing that integrity, intelligence, diligence, and some good fortune would lead to success. This was not always the case, of course, but a remarkable number of Jewish pioneers became prominent merchants, business leaders, and bankers. Jews were also elected to public office at nearly every level, despite forming a small portion of the electorate, and were well represented in private clubs.

Jewish merchants played an essential, if not always celebrated, role in the Gold Rush. Scores of mostly unprepared and untrained men headed to the gold mining areas, each of them needing food, cookware, clothing, blankets, boots, picks, shovels, pans, and so on. Invoices and freight papers from the period show that Jewish importers, wholesalers, distributors, and manufacturers dealt mainly with each other, forming a fluid network and highly efficient chain of supply. Jewish businesses were known to be stocked with the right merchandise at the right time and at reasonable prices.

During the early years, California Jews tended to be less religious than those who stayed in Europe or on the East Coast. Pious Jews needed close-knit communities with access to kosher food, a *mikvah* (ritual bath), and a synagogue within walking distance. Most Western Jewish settlers only attended services during the High Holidays (Rosh Hashanah and Yom Kippur), often in a private home and using a printed Torah. They were more likely to set up cemeteries and burial societies than synagogues. According to Jewish law, prayer services, festivals, and weddings can be performed without a professional leader or synagogue building. However, the dead must be prepared for burial in accordance with Jewish law and interred in specially consecrated ground. Hebrew Benevolent Societies assumed these responsibilities, establishing pioneer cemeteries in the Gold Rush towns such as Marysville, Grass Valley, Nevada City, Placerville, Jackson, Mokelumne Hill, and Sonora.

As Jewish communities began to take shape, so did congregations, fraternal lodges, and charitable organizations. Young men, who often ventured west alone, began marrying and settling down. By the 1870s and 1880s, many of these Jewish families had relocated to growing urban centers, such as San Francisco and Los Angeles, which provided better opportunities for education, stable work, and cultural enrichment. Other families remained in the Gold Country, relocating from town to town until finding steady communities.

The images in this book capture the Jewish pioneer experience in 12 California counties: Siskiyou, Modoc, Shasta, Butte, Yuba, Nevada, El Dorado, Amador, Calaveras, Tuolumne, Sacramento, and San Joaquin. They include the northern and southern mining areas, as well as adjacent towns and cities that supplied those mines. The geography is thus larger than what some might consider the Gold Country. However, because Jewish settlers were primarily engaged as merchants and suppliers, rather than miners, it is appropriate to include the "gateways" along with the Gold Rush towns.

This story is, by necessity, representative rather than comprehensive. The expansiveness of the landscape, transient nature of the people involved, and limited number of photographs available preclude a thorough history. Nevertheless, the existing images provide a compelling portrait of an industrious and adaptive immigrant population whose impact in the region is felt to this day. Theirs is a story of what happened when a historically persecuted people arrived in a strange new land where almost no one cared about their religion or place of origin.

# One

# SISKIYOU, MODOC, AND SHASTA COUNTIES

Jewish involvement in the northern Gold Country was linked to the profitability of the mines and the communities that formed around them. When mines went dry and new strikes were discovered elsewhere, Jewish merchants and their families had little trouble relocating to new communities. Following a gold strike in 1851 near what is today Yreka, prospectors flooded the region. The resulting economic and population boom prompted the creation of Siskiyou County on March 22, 1852. Directly east of Siskiyou, Modoc County occupies the far northeast corner of the state. The region attracted national attention in 1872–1873 when the US Army and indigenous Modoc people, for whom the county is named, engaged in protracted battles known as the Modoc War (or Lava Bed War)—the only major Indian war fought in California. The Modoc warriors were eventually captured, the "instigators" were executed, and more than 150 were exiled to the Quapaw Agency in Oklahoma. White settlement of Modoc increased with the expansion of its gold, timber, agriculture, and railroad industries, and the county was formed on February 17, 1874. Just south of Siskiyou and Modoc is Shasta County, established as one of the state's original counties in 1850. The county is named for Mount Shasta, which derives from the Shasta people, who were ethnically cleansed from the area. During the Gold Rush, the town of Shasta was a major supplier for northern prospectors and was called the "Queen City of the Northern Mines."

Photographer Louis Herman Heller was born in Hesse-Darmstadt, Germany, in 1839. After arriving in New York at age 16, he became an assistant to Julius Bien, a lithographer, fellow German Jew, and the first great scientific map engraver in the United States. Heller then set out on his own, joining the westward migration and arriving in Northern California around 1862.

By 1864, Louis Heller had settled in Yreka, Siskiyou County, near the Oregon border. He opened Yreka Photograph Gallery on Miner Street, where he sold ambrotypes, melainotypes, and cartes de visite, such as the one shown here. He also traveled with a photo-tent gallery to nearby rural areas, such as Sawyer's Bar, Happy Camp, and Rough & Ready (now Etna). In early 1869, he relocated to Fort Jones, where he remained until 1900.

Louis Heller photographed the Modoc War of 1872–1873, which pitted a band of roughly 55 Modoc against 1,000 US Army soldiers. The initial confrontation occurred in November 1872 and there were casualties on both sides. The Modoc fighters, under Captain Jack (Kintpuash), retreated to what is now Lava Beds National Monument, where they repelled the Army for seven long months. As the only Indian war to take place within California's borders, the conflict attracted national and international coverage. Heller took this stereograph of the Army camp at the Lava Beds. The stereoscopic technique creates the illusion of depth by presenting two offset images separately to the left and right eyes. When seen through a special viewer, the two-dimensional images combine to give the impression of a single three-dimensional image. Stereographs and cartes de visite were largely responsible for popularizing photography during this period.

On April 11, 1873, Modoc warriors murdered two US peace commissioners after the government refused Modoc demands for a reservation along the Lost River and exoneration for earlier murders of white settlers. The public was frustrated by the Army's inability to resolve the conflict. At a demonstration in Yreka, the secretary of the interior, Columbus Delano, was hanged in effigy. Louis Heller was there to photograph the scene, producing the earliest known image related to the Modoc War. A week later, Heller headed to the front lines with his stereoscopic camera. The exact dates of his Modoc War photographs are unknown. However, he returned to Fort Jones around May 5, 1873, with some 24 stereographs. Although he was present for much of the fighting, none of the photographs captured scenes of combat.

Warm Springs Indian scouts from Oregon served the US Army during the Modoc War. Louis Heller's photographs of the scouts and Army soldiers sold briskly, as predicted by the *Yreka Journal* of May 14, 1873: "they will undoubtedly sell with a rush, as everyone wants to see what the lava beds looks like, and to form an idea of the hard place soldiers have been obliged to fight the Indians in."

CAPTAIN JACK.

I certify that L. HELLER has this day taken the Photographs of the above Modoc Indian, prisoner under my charge.
Capt. O. B. THROCKMORTON, 4th U. S. Artillery, Officer of the Day.
I am cognizant of the above fact. GEN. JEFF. C. DAVIS, U. S. A.

During the months-long campaign, some of the Modoc continued fighting while others began to surrender. Captain Jack evaded capture until he was finally turned in by fellow Modoc on June 1, 1873. Louis Heller produced this iconic portrait of Captain Jack, who was tried in a military court and hanged on October 3, 1873.

13

Scarface Charley is thought to have fired the first shot at the Battle of Lost River, initiating the Modoc War. After the execution of Captain Jack, the tribe was exiled to Oklahoma and Scarface was appointed chief. Louis Heller took this portrait.

At first, Louis Heller's Modoc War stereographs were printed under his own name. However, he soon arranged to have them printed and distributed by Carleton Watkins's San Francisco–based Yosemite Art Gallery, a competitor of Eadweard Muybridge's distributor, Bradley & Rulofson. Muybridge, the famed pioneer of stop-motion photography and motion-picture projection, also took photographs of the Modoc War.

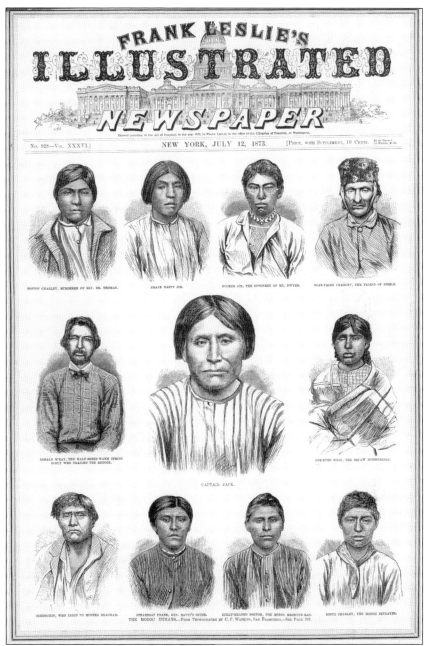

Louis Heller's portraits of Modoc captives sold widely through Watkins's Yosemite Art Gallery. His photographs appeared in *Harper's Weekly*, *Frank Leslie's Illustrated Newspaper*, and other publications. Unfortunately, photo credit was given to Carleton Watkins, even though Heller was the first to photograph the battle site, the first to have photos of the war appear in national publications, and the first to photograph Modoc captives. Years later, in 1889, the longtime bachelor married Alice Daggett, sister of former California lieutenant governor John Daggett. In August 1900, Louis and Alice placed their home, photography studio, and much of their personal property on the auction block. Before leaving Fort Jones for San Francisco, Louis destroyed all of his glass-plate negatives, believing them to be of no value.

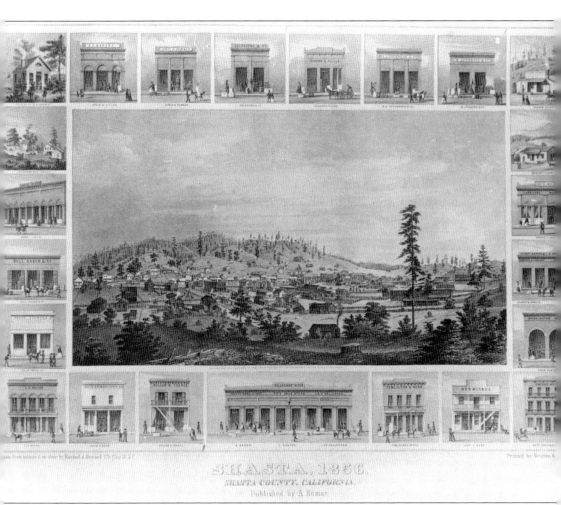

SHASTA, 1856.
SHASTA COUNTY, CALIFORNIA.
Published by A. Roman

Gold was discovered in Shasta County in the spring of 1848. As word spread, gold-seekers rushed into the area, followed by merchants who supplied the miners. According to the California state census of 1852, the county's population had grown to 4,050. When mining began to wane in the 1860s, boomtowns like Shasta gradually declined into ghost towns. Most of Shasta's Jewish residents were European-born merchants. Several of them had stores in the business district, while others operated from outlying areas, such as Horsetown, Cottonwood, and Weaverville. This illustration depicts Shasta in 1856, when it was the bustling county seat (a position occupied by Redding since 1887). The drawing includes three stores with Jewish names: Goldstone & Co., B. Jacobson & Co., and Hollub & Isaacs. Many of Shasta's Jewish-owned businesses were underwritten by partners in San Francisco.

This lithograph of the town of Shasta, produced in 1851–1852, depicts prospectors loading up on supplies. Among the stores pictured is that of J. Friedman, a Jewish merchant. The stores were as impermanent as the miners. As gold strikes gave out and new mines opened elsewhere, miners moved on and merchants either followed or left for San Francisco, where many of them had started out. Mobility was key to the success of Jewish merchants, who navigated the precarious economy by selling their inventories, changing business partners, and reestablishing themselves elsewhere. Unfortunately, this flexibility also makes tracing the history of Jewish businesses difficult, especially as newspapers tended to use a variety of spellings when reporting on business dealings. In general, merchants with recognizably Jewish names are considered to be Jewish, whether or not they were involved in a Jewish organization.

Adolphus Hollub, a San Francisco resident, partnered with Joseph Isaacs in a dry goods and clothing store in Shasta. Hollub did the buying for the Shasta store from San Francisco, and sold farm produce and gold dust taken in trade at the store. During the late 1850s and early 1860s, he was engaged in fur importing with S. Konalsky and S. Silverstone.

The original wooden store of Hollub & Isaacs burned down in a massive fire in June 1853 that leveled Shasta's business district. In October of that year, the store was moved to a fireproof two-story building. An advertisement in the *Yreka Mountain Herald* described the new store as a "fashionable dry goods and clothing emporium with goods just arrived to Shasta and adapted to the wants of this mining region."

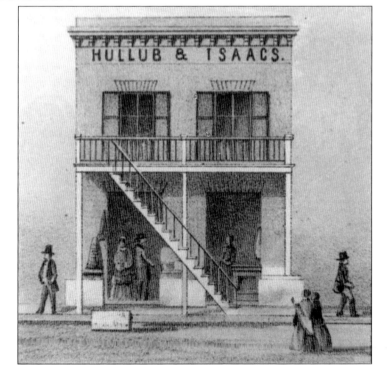

The ruins of the Hollub & Isaacs brick building still stand in the Shasta ghost town (Shasta State Historic Park), where the business once supplied miners and residents with fancy and staple dry goods, clothing, boots, shoes, queensware, cigars, and playing cards at wholesale and retail. Stores like Hollub & Isaacs helped make Shasta a major supply depot for mule trains heading to the northern mines. During its peak, 100 mule trains would stop in Shasta in a single night. This ended with the arrival of the railroad in 1888. Because of its many brick buildings, a sign of the merchants' commitment to the area, Shasta is one of the state's best-preserved ghost towns. The centerpiece of the Shasta State Historic Park is a fully restored county courthouse, which displays historical exhibits and artwork.

The Jacobson name figures prominently among Shasta's pioneer Jewish merchants. A ruined brick building in the Shasta State Historic Park bears the marker M. Jacobson and Co. Clothing. This 1856 drawing shows B. Jacobson & Co., a seller of ready-made clothing. H. Jacobson is also mentioned in local advertisements from that period.

The Goldstones were another of Shasta's prominent Jewish merchant families. Brothers Louis and Samuel Goldstone ran a clothing and dry goods business that burned down in June 1853. By July of the following year, they were operating out of a new brick building under the name Goldstone & Co.

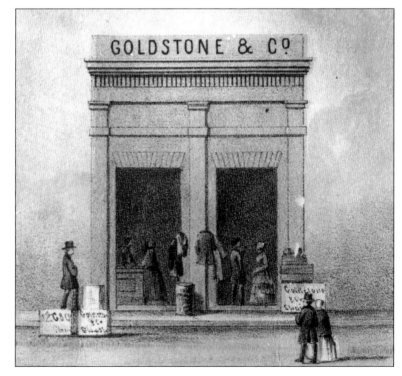

As the Goldstone brothers' business grew, Samuel ran the store in Shasta while Louis acted as the purchasing agent in San Francisco. By 1856, they were advertising business connections with Goldstone & Friedlander in New York and Goldstone, Friedlander & Co. in San Francisco. However, the firm was sold in October 1856 to Kady Gambitz, who continued at the same location for about a year.

In 1857, Michael Goldstone of San Francisco and Charles Goldstone of Shasta purchased the brick store still owned by Louis Goldstone. They renamed the company, which specialized in men's furnishings, M. & C. Goldstone. Today, the site is marked with a sign at the Shasta State Historic Park.

The A. & S. Solomon Co. sold ready-made clothes. The store's front and sides remain intact, making it among the best-preserved buildings at the Shasta State Historic Park. The store had three entrances, which are still guarded by iron doors and framed by decorative columns.

GRAVE OF PIONEER CHILD
*TRANSLATION OF HEBREW TEXT*

There is an exact correspondence between the information in the Hebrew text and that in the English text. The Hebrew date in the Hebrew text is accurate.

HEBREW
Here lies buried
the boy
Elchanan son of Eliakim
Broinshtein
from the city of
Red Bluff

Born on the 20th day of the month of 2d Adair in the year 5624 and died the 15th day of Kislev in the year 5625. From the creation of the world — (according to the Hebrew calendar).

ENGLISH
Charles
son of
George & Helena Brownstein
Born April 6, 1864
Died December 14, 1864

The name Brownstein survives in the Hebrew text as if it were pronounced Broinshtein.

In 1857, a group of Jewish merchants formed Shasta's Hebrew Benevolent Society. Their main objective was to bury Jewish pioneers in accordance with religious customs. George and Helena Brownstein of Red Bluff lost their eight-month-old son Charles on December 14, 1864. Because there was no Jewish burial ground in Red Bluff, the parents made the arduous journey to bury Charles in Shasta.

פנ
הילד אלחנן בן אל
ברוינשטיין
מעירן
רעד לופֿף
כולד ביום כמ לחדש אדר שני בשנת תרדכד
ונפטר טו כסליו בשנת תרכה
לפק
CHARLES
Son of
George & Helena Brownstein
OF RED BLUFF
Born April 6, 1864
Died Dec. 14, 1864

Although the Jewish cemetery of Shasta eventually disappeared, the grave of Charles Brownstein still remains. The gravesite was rediscovered in 1923 by a crew working on what would become Highway 299. The highway was rerouted to preserve the site, and was later widened south of the gravesite in 1933 and north of it in 1946. After the Redding Jewish Community Center was established in 1976, members volunteered to maintain the site and occasionally gathered there for services. In 1988, the tombstone was broken at the base and stolen. Although it was quickly recovered, the damage and years of weathering required a new tombstone to be fashioned. In 1990, the site was made a California Registered Historical Landmark with underwriting from E Campus Vitus, a fraternal society dedicated to the preservation of the heritage of the Mother Lode and gold mining regions of the American West.

Prussian-born businessman Simon Seelig was active in Shasta from 1855 to 1861. An 1855 newspaper commended his first business, with a Mr. Morris, for stocking California-grown "oranges and grapes decidedly superior in quality and flavor to any we have seen in this place." By July 1856, Seelig's Tobacco & Cigar store was occupying a new brick building. In March 1857, Seelig partnered with H. Newbauer, late of Greenwood & Newbauer in Weaverville, California. Newbauer worked from San Francisco, where he added to their stock of crockery, glass, tobacco, cigars, fruits, and nuts. When the company dissolved in 1858, Seelig entered a new tobacco business, Seelig & Levy. News of the Civil War reached Shasta in 1861, prompting Seelig to join the Union Army. After the war, he joined Adolphus Hollub in San Francisco in an oil and lamp business.

# *Two*
# BUTTE COUNTY

Butte County in California's Central Valley was incorporated in 1850 as one of California's original counties. The first gold strike in the region took place in 1848 in the town of Hamilton, which was briefly made the county seat—a position since occupied by Oroville. When gold was discovered along the Feather River in 1849, the area became a magnet for miners who staked out claims along the riverbanks. Businesses were opened nearby, and a community quickly emerged. Oroville was originally called Ophir City, after the biblical site of King Solomon's mine. However, a post office in another town had already taken that name, so Oroville was chosen instead, after *oro*, the Spanish word for gold. The mining town of Magalia was formed 20 miles north of Oroville. Gold was discovered there in 1851, and eight years later, a 54-pound nugget was unearthed at the West Branch of the Feather River. News of this discovery made the "lovely camp" one of Butte County's most important sites in the 1860s. Fifteen miles southwest of Magalia is the city of Chico. Founded by Gen. John Bidwell in 1860, Chico was conceived as a resting spot for weary travelers. With the arrival of enterprising settlers and the California and Oregon Railroad, Chico became a major agricultural supplier for the surrounding areas. Jewish settlers of Butte County followed patterns seen elsewhere in the Gold Country. Attracted to the area's mining economy, the mostly young immigrants—many of whom had relatives in San Francisco—took to selling clothes, dry goods, boots, shoes, tobacco, cigars, and other supplies. By the early 20th century, some would become wealthy landowners and developers of hotels and office buildings.

Originally from Mecklenburg-Schwerin in northern Germany, Edward A. Kusel reached New York in the early 1850s and soon after ventured to California. He arrived in Placerville in 1852 and worked as an upholsterer in Sacramento until a fire swept through the city, forcing him to move to a tent. When a flood devastated Sacramento, Kusel relocated to Marysville, where he made canvas hoses for miners on a sewing machine. Interested in the new art of photography, he opened a gallery in downtown Marysville above a theater before settling in Oroville in 1856. From Oroville, he maintained the Marysville store, opened photographic galleries in Chico and Sacramento, and expanded his business interests. An advertisement in the July 4, 1860, *Marysville Appeal* boasted that his gallery took ambrotypes, photographs, and solar pictures "copied, reduced, and enlarged in the best style of the art."

Edward Kusel maintained his photographic galleries between 1860 and 1870. After leaving the photography business, he opened a stationery and cigar store in Oroville. He gradually stopped selling cigars to concentrate on the stationery and variety shop items. In 1876, a two-story building was erected to house this store. Two years later, his eldest son, Carl Kusel, became a partner in the business. The store was renamed E. A. Kusel & Son. Despite only reaching the third grade, Edward was active in Oroville's civic, political, and educational affairs. An avid reader on a variety of subjects, he accumulated a large and eclectic library. A newspaper article from 1903 noted that he had donated 60 books for young people to the Oroville Public Library.

Edward Kusel married Bertha Heilbronner around 1856. The Kusel family, which grew to include four sons and a daughter, was greatly invested in the Oroville community. Edward was a school board trustee for 35 years and spearheaded the construction of the town's first schoolhouse. He was also an active abolitionist with the local chapter of the Union League, and contributed generously to Reform Judaism's Union of American Hebrew Congregations.

A devastating flood hit Oroville in March 1907. Forced from their home, the Kusels stayed at the Union Hotel, where Edward died of pneumonia. He was buried in the family plot at Oroville's Jewish Cemetery. The Kusel children contributed to Oroville for decades. Carl was elected mayor twice in 1907 and 1915. Eli, the youngest of the sons, was a respected medical doctor and helped found the Oroville Curran Hospital.

Established by merchant Henry Reilinger on April 5, 1859, the Jewish Cemetery in Oroville was deeded to the Hebrew Benevolent Society for $25. Twelve years later, on April 11, 1871, a second deed was filed by Andrew Gardella, a non-Jewish property owner. For $10, Gardella deeded the cemetery to businessmen Daniel N. Friesleben and Benjamin Marks. It is unknown how Gardella acquired the property after it had been deeded to the Hebrew Benevolent Society.

The earliest burials at Oroville's Jewish Cemetery took place in 1862, including Ellen Brooks, a daughter of state assemblyman Max Brooks. Ellen is buried alongside two siblings, Lawrence and Hannah. Their headstones attest to the high infant and child mortality rates of the period.

A native of Bohemia, Daniel N. Friesleben arrived in California in 1854 at age 22. Following short stints in San Francisco, Camptonville (Yuba County), Sutter County, and Marysville, Friesleben arrived in Oroville in 1857, establishing a general store, a hat and cap store, and a boot and shoe store. He also sold sewing machines, life insurance, and fire insurance. His properties included the Union Hotel and a 1,800-acre ranch, pictured here.

Daniel Friesleben died on January 25, 1897. He was buried in the family plot at Oroville's Jewish Cemetery, where his mother, both of his wives, and all but one of his children are also interred. The *Oroville Daily Register* reported, "In the death of D. N. Friesleben, Oroville loses a warm friend, an energetic citizen, a zealous partisan for her interests and her wealthiest businessman."

The earliest Jewish pioneers arrived in Chico during the 1860s and 1870s. Hailing from small towns in Germany, Poland, and Russia, the largely uneducated and penniless immigrants took to peddling. Many of the young settlers hailed from the same Polish town, Kempen, and had relatives nearby or in San Francisco. Some became small shopkeepers, specializing in dry goods, clothing, tobacco, and candy. By the early 20th century, a few had become wealthy owners of land, hotels, and office buildings. At the time, Chico's residents were predominantly Methodist, politically conservative, and agriculturally oriented, as exemplified by founder John Bidwell and his wife, Annie. Bidwell's contact with local Jews was limited to business matters. On at least two occasions, he sold property to men with Jewish names: on January 25, 1861, to Markus & King, and on December 14, 1868, to Elias Nathan.

Polish-born Herman Silberstein arrived in Chico in 1877, where he worked as a peach-picker at John Bidwell's expansive Rancho Chico. After a year, Silberstein had saved enough money to send for his family. He and his wife, Yettle (née Osroski), opened a small cigar stand on Broadway between Second and Third Streets, which they expanded to a men's furnishing store. The store later moved to Third Street. Herman and Yettle purchased properties and erected buildings, including the three-story La Grande Hotel in downtown Chico, which is listed in the National Register of Historic Places. Now known as the Silberstein Park Building, across from Chico's City Plaza, the structure was designed as an office building, despite being used as the Lyric Theatre and for many years as La Grande Hotel. The hotel ceased operations in 1981 and was refurbished in 1984.

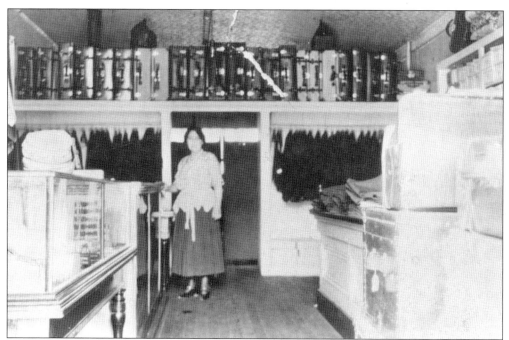

Barnett and Tillie Puritz, both Russian immigrants, arrived in Chico in 1911. They established a clothing store on Main Street, pictured here, and entered the junk business during World War I. The couple ventured into the oil industry in the mid-1920s. B. Puritz Oil Co., a two-pump gas station, was established around 1927.

Oroville's Jewish cemetery was the only such funerary ground in Butte County. As a result, a number of Chico residents were buried there, including Barnett and Tille Puritz. The cemetery houses a plaque donated by Congregation Beth Israel of Chico, honoring the memory of "those original Jewish settlers" who were drawn to the area during the Gold Rush.

*Main-Street Magalia*

Thousands of miners, cattle ranchers, woodsmen, and Chinese laborers resided in Magalia during the mid-19th century. Jews were among the town's leading shopkeepers. However, despite the influx of gold-seekers, the town was too small to warrant a separate post office building. Instead, the postmaster was chosen from the local merchants, who maintained a small post office in the corner of a store or hotel. The position was not well compensated, but having a post office in a store attracted foot traffic. Early Magalia had four Jewish postmasters who served a combined 37 years, beginning in 1867: Simon Marks, Hirsch Cohn, Levi Cohn (Hirsch's son), and Max Goodday (Hirsch's son-in law). The Cohn-Goodday store is pictured on the left.

Hirsch Cohn, a native of Poland, arrived in California with his brother Simon in 1848, and was later joined by his wife and three children. Hirsch began as a peddler, then purchased a horse-drawn wagon, and eventually obtained properties in the Sierra Nevada towns of Magalia, Lovelock, and Paradise, as well as in Biggs in the Sacramento Valley. His first store was in Magalia, pictured on the far left.

Following the death of his wife, Hirsch Cohn sold his Magalia store to his son Levi, the first of his children to be born in California. Levi was assisted by his younger brother Abraham until partnering with Max Goodday, who was married to Levi's older sister Lena. Levi Cohn is second from the left in front of the Cohn-Goodday store in this c. 1900 photograph.

The Cohn family purchased a number of properties, including the site of the Kunkle Reservoir and the Little Frog and Jerusalem mines. Forty acres of Levi Cohn's land were sold to the Paradise Irrigation District, which was later home to the Feather River Sanitarium. Levi and Bertha Cohn are pictured here with their daughters Norma and Hortense.

The Cohn-Goodday store attracted early automobile enthusiasts, as seen in this c. 1915 photograph. The store, described as a modest frame building with large cellars, a post office, and a barn for the storage of grain and hay, remained a fixture of the community until it was destroyed in a fire several years later.

Of the four Jews who served as postmaster of Magalia, Max Gooday's tenure was by far the longest. He held the position for 20 years, 1895 to 1915, compared to Simon Marks's six and a half years, Hirsch Cohn's three years, and Levi Cohn's eight years. Meanwhile, Gooday and Levi Cohn became the main suppliers of the area's mines, which numbered more than 50 during the peak years. They were also part owners of the Oro Fino Mine, a 270-acre drift mine approximately six miles northwest of Magalia, as well as other mining interests. Gooday purchased one of Magalia's first automobiles in 1913, five years after the Ford Motor Company debuted the Model T. He is pictured here behind the wheel, with Levi Cohn standing in front of the store, fourth from left.

The Cohn-Goodday store sold a variety of items, including hardware, dry goods, and groceries. Because of its wide variety, the business was called an "emporium." A miner is seen here loading his horses with goods as the Cohn daughters, Norma and Hortense, look on. The store also engaged in quasi-banking functions, accepting gold dust from miners for credit, and the Cohn family sometimes acquired land as payment for debts. The Cohns also occasionally sold off properties to satisfy creditors. Levi Cohn and Max Gooday ran the Magalia store until it was destroyed by a fire. Both men relocated to Chico, where Gooday operated a cigar and tobacco business. His wife, Lena, and their three children opted to live in San Francisco.

# *Three*

# Yuba, Nevada, and Placer Counties

Founded on February 18, 1850, as one of California's original counties, Yuba County is named for the Yuba River, a tributary of the Feather River in the Sierra Nevada and eastern Sacramento Valley. The river derives its name from an indigenous Maidu village called "Yubu" in early records, which may have been a variant spelling of the Spanish *uva*, meaning grape, as grape vines were found along the riverbanks. Marysville, Yuba's county seat, was a main supply town to the Gold Country. Jews began arriving in the area in the 1850s, and many stayed to become successful business owners. High Holidays were observed in Marysville in 1853. Two years later, the Marysville Hebrew Benevolent Society purchased land for the Marysville Hebrew Cemetery, followed by Congregation B'nai B'rith in 1857. During that period, a number of Jewish clerks and merchants joined the local lodge of the Independent Order of B'nai B'rith. Nevada County was formed in 1851 from the eastern portion of Yuba County. The county's name, meaning "snowfall" in Spanish, originated from a major snow storm that blanketed the area in 1850. Nevada City, the county seat, was the first California mining town with records of a Jewish religious ceremony, and High Holiday services were held at the town's Masonic Hall in 1852. Although Nevada City's Jewish residents numbered just 30, the services attracted coreligionists from nearby communities, such as Grass Valley and Rough and Ready. Placer County, created in 1851, lies just south of Nevada County. Its name derives from the Latin American Spanish term for sand and gravel deposits containing gold. There are accounts of a Jewish agricultural settlement in Placer County, about six miles from the town of Lincoln, beginning in 1909. Immigrants from Eastern Europe cooperatively farmed parcels of land there, mainly keeping orange groves.

The Marysville Hebrew Benevolent Society was active as early as 1852. The original bylaws stated, "The funds of the society shall be appropriated as follows: Relief to the poor, needy, sick, and the burial of the dead of the Hebrew persuasion in Marysville and vicinity." In 1855, the society purchased a square block to be dedicated as the Marysville Hebrew Cemetery. A high brick wall was erected around the cemetery, as well as a brick house used in connection with it. Before being abandoned in the early 1900s, the cemetery grew to about 50 headstones. Decades of neglect and flooding left the headstones toppled or damaged, as seen in this photograph from the early 1980s. Since 1995, the cemetery has been under the trusteeship of the Commission for the Preservation of Pioneer Jewish Cemeteries and Landmarks in the West.

The first Jewish burial in Marysville took place in 1850, just a year after the Gold Rush began. Samuel H. Goldstein was buried following his death at age 34 on May 30, 1850. His headstone identifies him as a "holy righteous man."

London-born Harry Barnett was buried in the Marysville Jewish Cemetery in 1873. A newspaper advertisement from 1860 promoted "H. Barnett's Grand Gift Enterprise" at the Marysville Theater. The event included "Grand Dramatic Entertainment" and "one of the most splendid assortments of Gifts ever presented at any Entertainment in the State."

Bavarian-born Simon Reinhart arrived in North America in 1859, first settling in Victoria, British Columbia. Together with Benjamin Reinhart, his brother and business partner, Simon moved to Elko, Nevada, and opened a store. Later that year, he relocated to Winnemucca, Nevada, establishing Reinhart Bros. general merchandise store, which the brothers operated along with their Elko location. Meanwhile, a third Reinhart brother, Eli, found his way to Marysville in 1865, where he ran a men's clothing store before joining Simon and Benjamin in Winnemucca. In 1872, Eli bought the interests of Benjamin and Simon and named the store E. Reinhart & Co. Following Eli's death in 1892, the company was run by Eli's nephews for several decades. It was considered the largest merchandising establishment in the state of Nevada.

Bamberger Bros. was among Grass Valley's Jewish-owned businesses. This receipt from 1882 lists a variety of fancy goods sold at the store. In August 1883, Bamberger Bros. announced its "grand liquidation sale" in the *Grass Valley Daily Union*, assuring readers that the brothers "resolved to discontinue business in Grass Valley, and therefore offer their large and well assorted stock of dry goods, carpets, etc., at a sacrifice: This sale is not sham, and will positively be continued until the last piece of goods is sold. . . . To enable us to enter soon into another branch of business elsewhere. Positively no goods sold on credit from this date, August 9, 1883. All those indebted to us will please call and settle." Ferdinand Bamberger and his wife, Susette, left Grass Valley for Southern California. They resided in San Diego until 1888 and then moved to Riverside, where Ferdinand opened a combination tobacco store and pool hall.

The Jewish cemetery of Grass Valley, known as Shaar Zedek (Gate of Righteousness), was established in 1856 by the town's Hebrew Benevolent Society (also called Shaar Zedek), and was later maintained by members of the local B'nai B'rith lodge. The first burial took place in 1857 and the last was recorded in 1891. At one time a five-acre plot, the site is now less than one acre. Louis Levy, born in Poland in 1839, was buried at the cemetery in August 1871. An inscription on his headstone reads, "Erected by his nieces and nephews." Many of the headstones, including Louis's, once stood upright, but weather and time caused them to fall flat on the ground. After years of neglect, the cemetery was acquired by the Commission for the Preservation of Pioneer Jewish Cemeteries and Landmarks in the West.

The Levy name was well represented in Grass Valley during the pioneer days. An 1861 directory lists several Levys, including S. Levy and a Levy in business with J. Morris. Abraham Levy, the son of Esther Levy of Victoria, British Columbia, died from tuberculosis on May 5, 1874, at the age of 23.

Maria B. Salaman died at five months and 26 days. She was the daughter of Abraham Salaman, a prosperous Grass Valley grocer. Clarence Morris Nathan was just two months and 16 days old when he died in 1874. His father, Nathan Nathan, had mine holdings and a clothing business.

Born in Metz, France, in 1800, Elie Halphen had been a captain in the French army and the mayor of Metz before political upheavals led him to California in 1852. After living in Oakland and Brown's Valley (Yuba County), Halphen settled in Grass Valley in 1867. He kept a saloon, had a shop, worked as a grocer, and held shares in a few mines.

**L. M. COHN**

HAS JUST OPENED HIS SPLENDID STOCK OF

**FALL AND WINTER GOODS,**

SUCH AS

**NEW DRESS GOODS,**

**NEW SILKS,**

**NEW DE LAINES,**

**NEW TRIMMINGS,**

**NEW BONNETS!**

Everything that is NEW and HANDSOME, at the **Lowest Prices** in the State.

**L. M. COHN,**

Philadelphia Store, Commercial street.

oc-23.

Despite being just four miles apart, Grass Valley and Nevada City maintained independent Jewish communities. Each town had its own Jewish religious organization, benevolent society, social and charitable groups, and cemetery. The unusual arrangement owed to the Gold Rush prosperity of both towns, which attracted a good number of Jewish businesses, including L.M. Cohn's store in Nevada City.

Nevada City had several highly valued Jewish-owned businesses, such as A. Block & Co. Writing in December 1852, the non-Jewish editor of the *Nevada Journal* remarked that Jews were among "our best citizens and merchants . . . men honest, peaceable and liberal, and good citizens in every sense of the term."

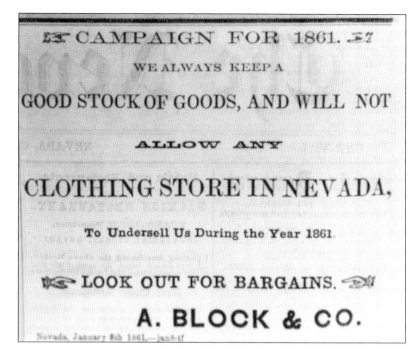

**CAMPAIGN FOR 1861.**

WE ALWAYS KEEP A

**GOOD STOCK OF GOODS, AND WILL NOT**

**ALLOW ANY**

**CLOTHING STORE IN NEVADA,**

To Undersell Us During the Year 1861.

**LOOK OUT FOR BARGAINS.**

**A. BLOCK & CO.**

Nevada, January 8th 1861—jan8-tf

Aaron Baruh arrived in Nevada City in 1854. He owned and operated the Family Grocery Store on Commercial Street. By 1867, he was also running a saloon on Commercial Street. He later owned the Jenny Ledge mining claim, which he named for his daughter. Baruh was active in the local Jewish community, serving as president of the Nevada Hebrew Benevolent Society (formerly Nevada Hebrew Society) in the mid-1860s.

Located at 516 Main Street in Nevada City, this house was built by Jacob Kohlman in 1852. Aaron Baruh purchased the house in 1866 for $585. The small frame structure includes two bedrooms and one bathroom. The children and grandchildren of Aaron and his wife, Theresa, were all born in the back bedroom. Aaron adorned each doorframe with a *mezuzah*, a decorative case holding a parchment with verses from the Torah. He also kept separate dishes for Passover and ordered matzah from San Francisco for the holiday. Many old belongings of the Baruh family were preserved in the house for generations. An outhouse, which had been attached to the house, was later detached and made into a toolshed.

David Baruh, the son of Aaron and Theresa, died in 1877 at the age of seven. He was interred at the Nevada City Jewish Cemetery, a 1.3-acre parcel acquired by the local Jewish community in 1854. In 1855, the Nevada Hebrew Society was organized "to hold religious services, maintain a burying ground for members and others, and assist the needy with pecuniary aid." The first burial took place the following year, and the last was recorded in 1890. The cemetery was dedicated as a historical site on October 29, 1972, and is accessible by a narrow road. Twenty-nine gravesites are currently visible, although some of them have been rendered illegible over time. The cemetery is now maintained by the Commission for the Preservation of Pioneer Jewish Cemeteries and Landmarks in the West.

The Baruh home remained in the family for nearly 150 years until being sold in 2014. The contents of the home were also sold, including furniture and jewelry from the 19th and early 20th centuries. The home is registered as a California Point of Historical Interest.

Benjamin Lachman was a miner before entering the hardware business with his brother Davis. Located on Commercial Street, D. & B. Lachman specialized in hardware, stoves, tinware, and crockery. Benjamin was also an original trustee of the Nevada Hebrew Society, which was founded on April 5, 1855, and met regularly on the first Monday of each month.

Jacob Lachman, the son of Benjamin and Dora Lachman, was just one month old when he died on June 3, 1859. He was interred in the Nevada City Jewish Cemetery. The Lachmans also lost seven other children, all of whom are buried in the cemetery. Two of them, Jennie and Joseph, died within two weeks of each other.

Rebecca Heyman died of suicide by drowning on February 16, 1874. Earlier that year, Rebecca, her husband, Solomon, and their son Gus were arrested and jailed for receiving and disposing of property stolen from freight cars of the Central Pacific Railroad. Rebecca posted bond and boarded a stage for Truckee to collect bail for her husband and son. However, she exited the coach about a half mile outside Nevada City and was later found in a shallow pool.

The last burial at the Nevada City Jewish Cemetery was that of Louis W. Dreyfuss, who died on July 22, 1890. Born in Germany in 1825, Dreyfuss arrived in Nevada City in 1851. At different times, he operated a saloon, the United States Bakery, and the Milwaukee Brewery, all on Pine Street. He was also elected the town's treasurer. Dreyfuss was a cousin of French army captain Alfred Dreyfus, of the infamous Dreyfus affair. His infant son Martin is also buried at the cemetery.

As mining operations declined in the decades following the initial Gold Rush, much of the Jewish population went elsewhere in search of better opportunities. German-born Mendel Esberg struggled to find work in Marysville and left for San Francisco, where he opened a cigar store on Kearny Street. Before long, he was manufacturing his own brands of cigars and later added stores in New York City; Portland, Oregon; and Havana, Cuba.

Abraham Blochman, a native of France, exemplified the mobility of California's pioneer Jews. Arriving in America with his siblings and widowed mother in 1848, Blochman clerked at a store in Helena, Arkansas, and taught French on the side before being drawn to the Gold Rush in 1851. He stayed in San Francisco and from there joined his brother Lazar in the gold mining region, clerking and trying placer mining along the Yuba River. In the spring of 1858, Abraham was elected secretary of the Nevada Hebrew Society. He later became a major business and ranching figure in San Luis Obispo and, from 1881, an important merchant, banker, and Jewish leader in San Diego. His sister Sarah was married to Jacob S. Landeker, who sold his Nevada City grocery store before moving the family to San Francisco.

Named by miners, the town of Last Chance is located high in the mountains of Placer County. By 1861, the town boasted 25 homes, 75 permanent residents, a butcher shop, and a sawmill. By 1884, it had grown to include seven saloons, a two-story hotel, and several stores. The *Last Chance Directory*, printed in 1861, describes harsh conditions in the mountain terrain: "During the winter season it is sometimes impossible for miners to obtain supplies, except by packing them themselves over the snow from Deadwood, a distance of seven miles. After the snows fall at the beginning of the winter season, it is sometimes months that the inhabitants have no communication with the lower world, except occasionally when an expressman travels over the snow to Michigan Bluff to procure letters and papers, which he takes to the people at the moderate charge of twenty-five cents for each letter and paper." Blue Eyes Mine, pictured here in 1882, was one of the area's attractions.

*Four*

# EL DORADO, AMADOR, AND CALAVERAS COUNTIES

Located entirely in the Sierra Nevada, El Dorado County was incorporated in 1850 as one of California's original counties. The land was the historic home of the Maidu, Washoe, and Miwok tribes. Named for the Spanish word for "golden," the area first attracted wide attention when gold was discovered at Sutter's Mill in Coloma in January 1848, setting off California's Gold Rush. The nearby town of Placerville was originally known as Dry Diggings, after the dirt-covered finds that had to be sorted with running water. The town was later called Hangtown, for a prominent hanging tree on the main street. When the town was incorporated in 1854, the name was changed to Placerville. The county seat since 1857, Placerville once had a Hebrew Benevolent Society, Ladies Hebrew Benevolent Society, Congregation B'nai B'rith, and Jewish cemetery. Amador County lies directly south of El Dorado County. Created in 1854 from parts of El Dorado and Calaveras Counties, the area was known as the "Heart of the Mother Lode." The county was named for José María Amador, a San Francisco–born rancher, soldier, and miner who established a successful mining operation near present-day Amador City. In 1857, B'nai Israel Congregation was formed in the town of Jackson, Amador's county seat. It was one of just two synagogues in the Gold Rush region, the other being in Placerville. Jackson also had a Jewish cemetery, known as Givoth Olam (Hills of Eternity). Calaveras County, which lies south of Amador County, is another of the state's original counties. Named for the Calaveras River, where Spanish explorer Gabriel Moraga found Native American skulls (*calaveras* in Spanish), the county is best known for Mark Twain's early short story, "The Celebrated Jumping Frog of Calaveras County" (1865). Mokelumne Hill, the county seat of Calaveras from 1852 to 1866, had a Hebrew Benevolent Society, Ladies Hebrew Benevolent Society, and Jewish cemetery. Members of its Jewish community contributed to the newly formed Hebrew Union College in Cincinnati, founded in 1875.

Samuel Sussman Snow left Germany for the United States in 1836 or 1837. While in New York City, he married Paulina Fink, whose Catholic family also came from Germany. After completing his medical degree at a French hospital, Snow headed west, engaging in the fur trade with indigenous people in Wisconsin and receiving his naturalization papers in St. Croix County, Wisconsin, in 1849. Samuel and Paula next acquired a land grant ranch in Council Bluffs, Iowa, where they intended to settle permanently. However, the cold winter of 1849–1850 disagreed with Paulina, who was pregnant, and the couple set out for California. Samuel helped to organize a wagon train and was chosen as its leader, no doubt because of his medical training and experience with Indians. He is the only Jew known to have led a covered wagon train from the Midwest to California. In August 1850, the wagon train arrived in Pleasant Valley, El Dorado County.

Paulina Snow was pregnant when she and Samuel left Iowa. Emanuel, their first child, was born during their 1850 trek to California. He later became a miner and a charter member of Placerville's Society of Territorial Pioneers. In 1925, during California's Diamond Jubilee, the state government honored him and other "covered wagon babies" born en route.

The Snows took squatters' rights on Sacramento land that was later the site of the state capitol. Samuel left his family there while he traded goods in Placerville and opened a tent store in nearby Dogtown. Once settled, he was joined by Paulina and Emanuel. The family acquired a mine in 1851 that produced gold for almost 100 years.

Paulina Snow was one of eight children born to Elisabeth Wagner and her first husband, Gallus Fink. She was christened on June 23, 1827, in the Catholic church in Fützen, Germany. Despite her Catholic upbringing, Paulina was not inclined to carry on her family's religion. Samuel ensured that their children were raised with Jewish customs, despite the unavailability of formal Jewish education. The couple had nine children: Emanuel, Joseph, Jacob, Benjamin, Carrie (Caroline), Herman, Emily, Charles, and Jennie (who died in infancy). They were active in Placerville's Hebrew Benevolent Society and Hebrew synagogue. Three of Paulina's siblings also settled in California. Her sister Sophia and brother John are buried at the Pleasant Valley Cemetery in El Dorado County, and her brother Charles is interred at Arroyo Grande Cemetery in San Luis Obispo County.

The community of Iowaville, about nine miles east of Placerville, was established around 1850. It once had as many as 600 residents, but it faded into a ghost town by the 1880s. In 1851 or 1852, Samuel Snow purchased an Iowaville ranch house along Pleasant Valley Road. The building, erected in 1850 with imported Georgia pine, had living quarters for the family upstairs and a store and bowling alley downstairs. Livestock were branded with a double-S. Samuel, and later his sons, continued purchasing adjacent land until the family owned 1,200 acres from Camino Ridge to Newtown. Jacob Snow built a residence on the ranch in 1906, just south of the North Fork of Weber Creek. The new structure incorporated lumber from old buildings on the family ranch.

Two of the Snow children, Herman and Carrie, are pictured here. Herman was stricken with polio at age 15. The disease was poorly understood at the time, but Samuel wisely sent his son to Mexico, where the warm, dry climate helped him to regain his strength. Carrie later married Rabbi-Cantor Herman Davidson of Stockton.

Emily Snow, standing on the right next to her sister Carrie, grew up to marry Charles Davis. Emily died tragically on April 8, 1891, from complications following childbirth. A short while later, Samuel Snow was left partially paralyzed after suffering a stroke. His will, written after the stroke, includes Emily's baby Viola as a beneficiary in his estate.

Samuel Sussman Snow died on July 9, 1892. An obituary from an unidentified Placerville newspaper reads in part, "Mrs. Snow died about ten years ago. The family surviving the death of these parents is composed of six sons and one daughter, Miss Carrie Snow, now residing at Newtown. All are grown, and two sons now reside outside the county, one in San Francisco, another in Washington. The funeral occurred in this city last Monday afternoon, the remains being interred in the Jewish cemetery, where Mrs. Snow was also laid away for the final rest, years ago. There was a long train of carriages from the vicinity of the residence bearing neighbors who thus testified to their respect for the memory of the deceased. Mr. Snow was a man of much energy, intelligence and business sagacity, and many of his sterling traits of character are reproduced in the family of estimable young people he has left behind him."

At the time of his death in 1892, Samuel Snow's property holdings consisted of 365 acres in El Dorado County and a lot on Hayes Street in San Francisco, along with a $1,150 bank deposit, $500 worth of gold dust, and personal possessions such as furniture, wagons, wood, horses, and goats. Much of the real estate was auctioned off on July 13, 1895. The San Francisco lot was sold to Sarah Snow, Emanuel's wife, at a public auction. Records also show a payment of $40 to Rev. [Rabbi] Joseph Leonard Levy of Congregation B'nai Israel of Sacramento, who conducted Snow's funeral on July 11, 1892. The El Dorado County property included the water ditch and dam on the North Fork of Weber Creek. Members of the Snow family are pictured at the dam.

The Snow family's mining operations continued long after Samuel Snow's death in 1892. The Snow Consolidated Placer Mine (also known as Joseph Snow & Co. and Snow Brothers Mine) was a 300-acre hydraulic mine, which used high-pressure jets of water to dislodge rock material and move sediment. The mine became active around 1896, when cemented gravel was mined in two pits. Five miles of ditches were dug from the northern section of Weber Creek to the ranch house in Iowaville, providing 300 miner's inches of water (a measurement of the flow of water from a supply system, such as a flume or sluice). Large reservoirs were built just above the house to store water for the flumes. The open pits were mined as recently as the late 20th century.

The Placerville Jewish Cemetery was founded in 1854 by the local Hebrew Benevolent Society, of which Samuel Snow was a trustee. The first burial, for merchant Marcus Abraham, took place in 1856. During the same period, another Jewish cemetery was established in nearby Diamond Springs, but the site has not been identified. A Jewish congregation formed in Placerville in 1858, and property was acquired for a synagogue building in 1861 on Cottage and El Dorado Streets. The building was destroyed by a windstorm in 1878, and a second synagogue structure was abandoned in 1903. The Placerville Jewish Cemetery was active until 1968, when the last burial was conducted for George Yohalem, a New York native who retired from the motion picture business and ran Placerville's Pioneer Bookshop. The cemetery is now under trusteeship of the Commission for the Preservation of Pioneer Jewish Cemeteries and Landmarks in the West.

Paulina Snow is buried at the Placerville Jewish Cemetery. The *Placerville Mountain Democrat* reported on her sudden death at age 54: "Mrs. Paulina Snow, wife of Samuel Snow, one of the oldest and most respected residents of that section, and one in usual good health, apparently went to work on the week's washing. About ten o'clock she felt slightly unwell, lay down, commenced vomiting and about four o'clock, died."

The Snow family plot at the Placerville Jewish Cemetery includes Samuel, Paulina, and their sons Joseph, Herman, and Charles. The family continued its business dealings in mining, ranching, and lumber for several generations. Snows Road in Placerville is named for them.

A native of Exin, Prussia, Edward Cohn was a beloved member of Placerville's Independent Order of Odd Fellows Morning Star Lodge No. 20. The lodge published a memorial for Cohn in the *Mountain Democrat* on November 20, 1880. His tombstone depicts the ceremonial hand gesture of the Kohanic blessing.

Three-year-old Herman Landecker is one of several children buried at the Placerville Jewish Cemetery. His elaborate headstone features leafy adornments, two crossed ferns, and the phrase "Sheltered and safe from sorrow."

Augustus Mierson apprenticed at a dry goods store in his native Germany before leaving for London at age 19. During the Crimean War, he was contracted with an English firm to manufacture rubber overcoats. He sailed for New York in 1856, and from there headed west as a traveling salesman. Mierson arrived in San Francisco in 1860, securing employment as a store clerk. After accumulating sufficient funds, he relocated to Placerville, where he partnered with his brother-in-law Godfrey Jewell. Their business was first called Mierson and Jewell, then A. Mierson Banking Co., and later A. Mierson & Sons. Mierson served on the grand jury of El Dorado County during the 1860s and was recognized as one of the wealthiest citizens of the county. His son Max reorganized the bank in 1919; it was later acquired by Bank of America.

German-born Joseph Brandenstein arrived in California in 1850. He operated a short-lived dry goods business with Joseph P. Newark in Placerville before settling in San Francisco, where he opened a wholesale leaf tobacco and cigar business. In San Francisco, Brandenstein distinguished himself as a major figure in the German and Jewish communities. As president of the German Benevolent Society in the 1870s, he selected the site of the German hospital. He also founded the Altenheim, a German senior citizens' home, serving as its president for many years, and was on the board of the Pacific Hebrew Orphan Asylum and president of the Mt. Zion Hospital Association. He was an active member of the Eureka Benevolent Society and Congregation Emanu-El. Brandenstein retired from his tobacco business in 1880 to devote his life to philanthropic causes. In 1881, Max Joseph Brandenstein, Joseph's son, began the MJB coffee brand with assistance from his brothers Mannie, Charlie, and Eddie.

Congregation B'nai Israel of Jackson was organized for the High Holidays of 1856. The following fall, the congregation dedicated the first synagogue in the mining districts. The building was apparently only used during the High Holidays. By 1869, attendance for the annual services had outgrown the building, which was converted into a schoolhouse. Historical Landmark No. 865 commemorates the location, currently Jackson Grammar School.

The Jewish cemetery in Jackson, known as Givoth Olam (Hills of Eternity), was founded in 1857. The cemetery includes 32 visible gravesites and is surrounded by cypress trees and a wrought iron fence. The cemetery, which had its final burial in 1921, is under the trusteeship of the Commission for the Preservation of Pioneer Jewish Cemeteries and Landmarks in the West.

Rachel was the stillborn daughter of Mark and Fanny Levinsky. She was the first burial at Jackson's Givoth Olam cemetery in 1857. Her parents buried two other infants at the cemetery: Alphonse (1861), who was three years old, and Abraham (1862), who was a stillborn. John Levinsky, Mark's brother and business partner, also buried two children in Jackson: two-year-old Harriette Olga (1860) and stillborn Edith Rachel (1863).

Rachel Haines, a native of Prussia, arrived in Jackson with her sister. Rachel married Abraham Haines at the Jackson home of Herman Goldner, the proprietor of a variety store. Haines was one of several German-born brothers to settle in California in the 1850s and 1860s. The couple resided in El Dorado, where Rachel died at the age of 24. Her death is the first recorded for a Jewish resident of El Dorado.

Isaac Peiser immigrated to Jackson from Russia. Other members of the Peiser family are also interred at the Givoth Olam cemetery, including Isaac's seven-year-old son Abbie; Julius Peiser, who may have been Isaac's brother; and John von Peiser, the two-year-old son of T. and P. Peiser.

Hette Steckler, a native of Prussia, was the first wife of Charles Steckler, a Bohemian-born businessman. Charles was co-owner of a grocery business in Jackson before running saloons in Jackson and nearby Volcano. He later had a dry goods store where he advertised, "I sell Cheap for Cash Only." Charles and Caroline Steckler, likely Charles's second wife, are also buried in the Steckler family plot at Givoth Olam.

Born in Exin, Prussia, Miriam Cohn was the mother of Susan Samuels and the matriarch of the Samuels family of Jackson. Eighty-five years old when she died in 1882, she is buried at Givoth Olam alongside four small children of the Samuels family, including her grandsons Hyman and Samuel.

Mark Strouse, his parents, and a brother emigrated from Germany in 1860 and settled in Mokelumne Hill in the heart of California's Gold Country. Mark worked in the mining industry and the mercantile and butcher trades. In 1863, he relocated to Virginia City, Nevada, where he opened meat markets and developed a hog ranch.

The Mokelumne Hill Jewish Cemetery was established in 1859 by the local Hebrew Benevolent Society and Ladies Hebrew Benevolent Society. The first burial at the cemetery was that of Isaac Lurch, a native of Bavaria and a resident of Lancha Plana, a Gold Rush town south of Mokelumne Hill. The site, which is entered through the Protestant Cemetery, is maintained by the Commission for the Preservation of Pioneer Jewish Cemeteries and Landmarks in the West.

Erected in 1854, the stone front of the L. Mayer & Son store stands where Center and Main Streets meet in downtown Mokelumne Hill, just outside of the Jewish cemetery. The store is adjacent to the 1855 Wells Fargo office, which was originally Levinson's store.

Two structures down from L. Mayer & Son is the Independent Order of Odd Fellows (IOOF) Hall, also built in 1854. Originally the two-story home of the Adams Express Agency office, the stone structure was modified in 1861 to became the first three-story building in the Gold Country. The Odd Fellows originated in England and was first brought to the United States as a working-class society. By the 1840s, a middle-class element entered the fraternity, and by 1897, IOOF's American branch counted 810,000 members. Throughout the American West, Jewish men were often charter members of both the Odd Fellows and Masons, which had a civic focus during the pioneer days. Jewish communities regularly rented fraternal halls for religious observances.

German native Arnold Friedberger arrived in the United States in 1852. Five years later, he headed west to Sheep Ranch in Calaveras County, where he opened a general merchandise store. He later settled in San Andreas, where he had another store and, together with Dr. Robertson, purchased the site of Dr. Robertson's Drug Store on 50 North Main Street. Arnold and Lotta were married in 1867. The Friedberger family relocated to Stockton in 1882.

Born in 1826 in Baden, a historical territory in south Germany, Moses Dinkelspiel was a soldier in the King's Guards before rebelling and fleeing to France. He landed in New York City on July 4, 1848, and remained there until gold fever brought him to San Francisco via the Isthmus of Panama. Built in 1851, Dinkelspiel's General Merchandise store in Vallecito is the oldest known surviving store in Calaveras County.

After selling his Vallecito store in 1858, Moses Dinkelspiel relocated to Suisun, in Solano County, where he opened another general store and became active in politics. During more than a century of operation, the Vallecito store passed between six owners. The Arata family, which operated the store in the early 20th century, kept a large tank of gasoline for the few customers who needed it. Gas pumps were installed at the store in 1925. The building is still fully functional, complete with iron shutter doors, wood and masonry walls, wood ceilings, and concrete slab floors. The beautifully preserved structure, which bears an E Clampus Vitus historical marker, has since been converted to a private residence. The marker, dated September 14, 2002, notes that Dinkelspiel's store "was one of the many express companies which handled mail in the Mother Lode prior to 1854, when the post office was established."

## Five

# TUOLUMNE COUNTY

Created in 1850 as one of California's original counties, Tuolumne was known as Oro County prior to statehood. Parts of Tuolumne County were given to Stanislaus County in 1854 and to Alpine County in 1864. The eastern portion of the county includes the northern section of Yosemite National Park. Sonora, the county seat, was founded by miners from Sonora, Mexico, who began mining for gold there in 1848. News of a gold strike in 1849 spread to the East Coast and internationally. Scores of pioneers sailed to Panama, where they crossed the isthmus on foot or horseback and boarded crowded ships for San Francisco. From there, it was a two-day schooner trip to Stockton, followed by a stage coach through the foothills to Sonora. By 1849, the camp's population had increased to about 5,000, making it one of the largest mining towns in the Mother Lode. Mexican miners experienced brutal attacks in those early years, and beginning in 1850, were pushed out by harsh non-citizen taxes. The Hebrew Congregation of Sonora was formed in 1851 to accommodate High Holiday worshipers. Rather than building a synagogue, the congregation conducted services at homes and rented halls, such as the Odd Fellows building. In 1853, the Hebrew Congregation acquired land for the Sonora Hebrew Cemetery, the Gold Country's oldest Jewish cemetery. Sonora's Hebrew Benevolent Society began in 1856 and expanded to the Sonora and Columbia Hebrew Benevolent Society in 1859–1860. Known as the "Queen City of the Southern Mines," Sonora remained an important center for lumber, agriculture, and cattle after its mines were exhausted.

Born to French-Jewish immigrants in Philadelphia, attorney Henry A. Lyons arrived in Louisiana in the 1830s. He became a member of the bar in St. Francisville before leaving for California. In Sonora, he ran for the first California legislature in 1849, but was defeated. When the state's constitution was ratified in November 1849 in advance of statehood the following year, Lyons was selected for a four-year term on the three-man supreme court. When Chief Justice S.C. Hastings's two-year term expired in 1852, Lyons took his place. Despite his high position, he made few contributions to California's jurisprudence, writing just 11 opinions during his time on the state's supreme court. His interests were mostly social and commercial. When he died in San Francisco in 1872, he left an estate of nearly half a million dollars, an enormous sum in those days.

Avoiding military service in Poland, Michael Goldwater (Michel Goldvasser) spent several years in Paris and London before arriving in California in 1852. Two years later, he was in Sonora, where he was joined by his brother Joseph, his wife, Sarah, and the two small children they had at the time. Goldwater's impressive height of six feet, three inches earned him the nickname "Big Mike," while his shorter brother was called "Little Joe." Michael worked as a fruit dealer in Sonora, but after two years declared himself an "insolvent debtor." Likely because of his business problems, Sarah set up a tailoring and merchandising business in her own name. Michael served as vice president of the Sonora Hebrew Benevolent Society before moving to Los Angeles with his family and later settling in San Francisco. In 1896, the sons opened Goldwater's Department Store in Phoenix, Arizona. Michael was also the grandfather of Arizona senator Barry Goldwater.

Meyer Baer, a native of Hamburg, Germany, settled in Sonora in 1851, where he opened a crockery business in a tent. A short time later, he formed a clothing store with a Mr. Leszynsky. The partnership dissolved around 1858, but Meyer pressed on, establishing a successful clothing business with Moses Hannauer, who was a trustee of the Hebrew Benevolent Society. Baer also served as a lay rabbi for Sonora's Jewish community.

Helena Oppenheimer Baer, pictured here with her son Julius, was a native of Stolhofen, Germany. She was the wife of Meyer Baer and the sister-in-law of his business associate Moses Hannauer. Helena came to Sonora around 1859. She had eight children and held considerable property in her own name.

Meyer Baer's youngest son, Julius, ran his father's store during much of the 20th century. In 1909, two years after Meyer's death, Sonora's *Union Democrat* reported, "Ask the well-dressed men you meet where they bought their suits, shirts, ties or hats, and a nice percentage will reply, 'at Baer's'; some will say 'Julius Baer's,' because everybody knows the enterprising proprietor of the Washington Street establishment that has appropriately been named 'The Home of Good Clothes.' . . . At his father's death the junior partner, who had been largely instrumental in giving the store the splendid reputation and trade it enjoyed, succeeded to the business and has ever since been the sole proprietor." The original Baer's clothing store was just south of the store's location at 105 South Washington Street, which remained open until 1995. The store's logo had 1851 as the year of establishment, corresponding to Meyer Baer's arrival in Sonora and the start of his business ventures.

Julius Baer, pictured here at four years old, was born in 1877. In 1962, he became a trustee of the Sonora Hebrew Cemetery, which was the first Gold Rush Jewish cemetery when it was created in 1853. Two years after his death in 1972, the cemetery was rededicated as a historic site. It is currently maintained by the Commission for the Preservation of Pioneer Jewish Cemeteries and Landmarks in the West.

The Baer family plot at the Sonora Hebrew Cemetery includes Helena, Meyer, and daughter Daisy, whose names share a gravestone; daughter Mary, who had a millinery establishment; daughter Rebecca, who was a teacher and sweetshop proprietor; and daughter Fanny, who died at age two.

Polish-born businessman Emanuel Linoberg arrived in Sonora in the 1840s. In 1856, he built a stone and brick store at the northeast corner of today's Washington and Linoberg Streets. The structure, which had iron doors and shutters and a fireproof roof, was later used as a Wells Fargo office. Tension rods installed on the south side of the building were secured with letters spelling out the Linoberg name. By the time of his sudden death in 1858 at age 40, Linoberg had established himself as a successful merchant, participant in local politics, and past president of the Hebrew Congregation of Sonora. Although he did not engage in mining himself, he invested in various mining outfits, such as the South Carolina Quartz Mining Company. His other ventures included raising cattle and tobacco, manufacturing lime, and operating Russian steam baths at his ranch, which were recommended for the treatment of "stubborn ailments."

Accounts of Emanuel Linoberg's funeral attest to his esteem in the Sonora community. The *San Joaquin Republican* noted in March 1858, "His funeral was attended by the Masons, Odd Fellows, Hebrew Benevolent Society, Firemen, and a large number of citizens." Emanuel's widow, Pauline, later married his brother Louis, a resident of nearby Mariposa. They moved to San Jose, where Paulina owned a millinery shop.

Sonora had three main gold mines, including Bonanza, once considered the most productive pocket gold mine in the world. Charles Clark, a native of Delaware County, New York, was part owner of the Bonanza mine, along with James Divoll and Joseph Bray. They purchased the mine in the early 1870s. A major strike in 1879 yielded 990 pounds of gold in just one week.

Henry Leon Ferguson, the infant son of John and Rosalie, died after just 27 days. Another headstone in the family plot lists Henry and seven of his siblings: "Infant Son" (1888), Adele J. (1885–1898), Edna S. (1882–1911), Clara (1877–1889), Charles C. (1886–1904), Carl M. (1881–1911), and Frank L. (1891–1936).

German-born Moses Reeb worked as a miner before entering the clothing business and peddling throughout Tuolumne County. He eventually opened a shoe store in Sonora with his brother. A remembrance in the *Union Democrat* in June 1891 notes, "He was a man of indomitable will and perseverance, and by dint of hard labor and natural business tact he was successful in his business affairs."

George Morris was killed in a robbery while protecting his family store in Chinese Camp, Tuolumne County, which also housed a Wells Fargo office. The *San Francisco Call* of December 5, 1895 reported that "Albert and Wesley McReynolds, the supposed murderers of George Morris at Chinese Camp, four weeks ago, spent a quiet day in their separate cells in the County jail. Their precocious sister, Ada, is likewise in solitary confinement." The article continued, "Whoever the murderers were they may thank their stars first that they are not in the hands of the friends of popular George Morris. Again they may reconcile themselves that they failed to secure the sack of silver which Morris had just received." A bullet-pierced shutter from the Morris store is part of the Wells Fargo and Company Museum Collection. Morris's headstone is inscribed, "A Martyr to Duty."

In memory of
ISIDOR,
Son of Louis & Rachel
JACOBS.
Born Jun. 11, 1862,
Died May 4, 1869.

Seven-year-old Isidor Jacobs, the son of Louis and Rachel Jacobs, drowned on May 4, 1869, in a mined-out lot on Main Street in Sonora, near M. Rhem's Saloon, which had been filled with water. The boy was rocking from side to side in a small boat when he fell out. Other boys at the scene reportedly saw Isidor come up for air two or three times before sinking, at which time they "gave the alarm." The body was quickly fished out with a butcher's hook, but it was too late. Isidor's grave at the Sonora Hebrew Cemetery is surrounded by several others belonging to young children, a testament to the high rate of infant and child mortality in the pioneer period.

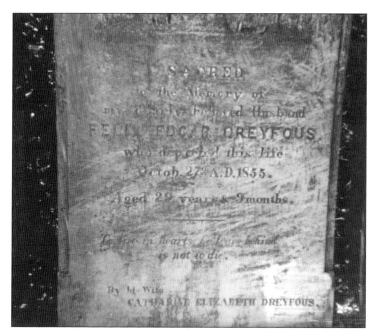

French-born Felix Edgar Dreyfous was married to Catherine Elizabeth (née Tindell) for just over eight months when he died at age 29. A merchant and auctioneer, Dreyfous had a store opposite Sonora's Long Tom Saloon. His headstone is inscribed, "Sacred to the memory of my dearly departed husband, Felix Edgar Dreyfous . . . to live in hearts we leave behind is not to die, by his wife, Catherine Elizabeth Dreyfous."

Sonora merchant Henry Cohen was a native of the Prussian province of Posen. His gravesite is enclosed by an ornamented wrought iron fence, and his headstone includes a popular verse from the Book of Ecclesiastes: "The dust shall return to the earth as it was; and the spirit shall return unto God who gave it" (12:7).

# PHILIP SCHWARTZ,

### WHOLESALE AND RETAIL

# FANCY DRY GOODS

.....AND....

# CLOTHING STORE.

## MAIN STREET,

### COLUMBIA.

---

OFFERS to the Ladies and gentlemen an extensive variety, of Fancy and Staple Goods, suited to their different wants. Having enjoyed a good patronage from the Ladies for the last three years, hopes by untiring exertions to be able to furnish them with the best and most desirable goods brought to the Pacific Shores.

Gentlemen will find every variety of furnishing goods, and at prices that cannot fail to please.

Columbia, just a few miles north of Sonora, began as a boomtown when gold was discovered in the vicinity in 1850. Thousands were drawn to the bustling locale, which by 1852 had eight hotels, four banks, two firehouses, two bookstores, three churches, a newspaper, over 40 drinking and gambling spots, and 17 general stores. Columbia became known as the "Gem of the Southern Mines," providing all types of entertainment and goods to miners in the area. Philip Schwartz was among the merchants who took advantage of the gold-driven economy. Advertisements for his Main Street clothing store promoted the volume and variety of selections. Schwartz called his business the New York Dry Goods Store, equating his merchandise with that found in the nation's premier city. In addition to owning and operating the store, he was a bonded collector for foreign miners' licenses.

## JOEL LEVY,

### DEALER IN

# CLOTHING & DRY GOODS,

## Corner Main and Fulton Streets,

### Columbia.

A large and Superior Stock of Gentlemen's Furnishing Goods always on hand, Miners' heavy Clothing, Rubber Coats, Pants, Boots, &c., &c.

Joel Levy's clothing store on Main and Fulton Streets in Columbia was known as both Levy's Store and Three Brothers' Store. Like Philip Schwartz, Levy filed bonds with the county to serve as a collector of foreign miners' licenses. He was also a lay service leader for the Jewish community of Columbia.

# SEGAR STORE:

## Ferguson's Block,

### COLUMBIA.

# I. NACHMANN,......Proprietor.

Keeps the best and finest article of SEGARS, TOBACCO. SNUFF, &c., in the Market, and solicits lovers of the Weed, to call, try, and judge for themselves. None but the Choicest will be offered for sale.

I. Nachmann's Segar Store was located in Ferguson's Block, a major commercial building in Columbia. Nachmann's store supplied miners with all their tobacco-related needs. The obsolete spelling of "cigar" in the store's name was already out of date when Nachmann opened his business in the 1850s.

*Six*

# SACRAMENTO COUNTY

Spanish cavalry officer Gabriel Moraga led expeditions into California's Central Valley between 1806 and 1808. Several of the names he bestowed to the region have survived, sometimes in anglicized or shortened forms, including Calaveras, San Joaquin, and Sacramento. The Sacramento River, for which both the county and county seat (and state capital) are named, derives from the Santisimo Sacramento (Holy Sacrament) of the Catholic Eucharist. The city of Sacramento owes its beginnings to John Sutter Jr., whose father operated Sutter's Mill in Coloma, where the Gold Rush began in January 1848. Thousands of gold-seekers converged on Coloma, many of them squatting on unwatched portions of Sutter's land. By December 1848, John Sutter Jr. and his associate John Brannan began laying out the city of Sacramento. Their main goal was to alleviate debt inflicted by prospectors who had absconded Sutter's belongings and land holdings in Coloma. Sacramento was the earliest incorporated city in California (February 27, 1850) and was made the state capital in 1854. Jewish settlement in the area began in 1849 with the arrival of European-born merchants. In 1852, Congregation B'nai Israel built the state's first synagogue building. The congregation's early rabbis traveled to mining towns to conduct services. Sacramento Jews also founded a Hebrew Benevolent Society, Ladies Hebrew Benevolent Society, B'nai B'rith Lodge, and Mosaic Law Congregation. The Sacramento County town of Folsom, best known for Folsom Prison (established in 1880), also attracted a number of Jewish merchants who accommodated the area's extensive placer-mining operations.

In 1849, Orthodox services were held at the Sacramento home of jewelry merchant Moses Hyman. Around the same time, Hyman helped form a Hebrew Benevolent Society together with Albert Priest, believed to be Sacramento's first Jewish settler. In 1852, a small frame building was purchased from the Methodist Episcopal Church to house Congregation B'nai Israel. Two months later, a fire destroyed much of the building.

Educated at Jews' College in London, Rabbi Barnett Elzas was one of many rabbis to serve Congregation B'nai Israel. Under his leadership from 1893 to 1894, the congregation continued its slow movement toward Reform Jewish practice, adopting the movement's *Union Prayer Book*. Members who preferred an older style of worship had broken away to form Mosaic Law Congregation in 1879.

Fires and floods were common in the early days of Congregation B'nai Israel. Between 1852 and 1904, the congregation occupied a number of buildings, some for as short as a year or two. The cornerstone for a more permanent home was laid in 1904 at 1421 Fifteenth Street. The new structure, which was paid for with funds raised by congregants, was consecrated in 1905. In 1912, a fire caused by an overheated basement stove nearly destroyed the building. The fire started while Sunday school was in session, but no one was hurt. The synagogue was renovated and reopened about a year later, and a new pipe organ was installed. The congregation remained there until 1954, when it moved to its current location at 3600 Riverside Boulevard. Through the decades, the campus has expanded to include a chapel, library, and education wing.

In 1850, Moses Hyman acquired land to create Home of Peace Cemetery. The cemetery was moved to its current site on Stockton Boulevard in 1924. Among the headstones is one belonging to German-born sisters Yetta and Bertha Kaiser. Bertha was the wife of Solomon Coney, a founding officer of Sacramento's Har Sinai Lodge No. 5 of the Ancient Jewish Order Kesher Shel Barzel (Band of Iron, established in 1865).

Helen Newmark (née Levinson), a native of Poland, married Joseph Newmark in Sacramento in the early 1860s. He was a cousin of Harris Newmark, the esteemed Los Angeles businessman, philanthropist, and historian. Helen wrote about the death of her son Herrman in her 1900 memoir: "He died when he was just four months old. This made a deep impression on my spirit; I felt as if I could never be joyous again."

Asher Hamburger and his two brothers, natives of Bavaria, arrived in Sacramento in 1850. Asher's brothers soon moved to San Francisco, where they formed a wholesale mercantile house. Asher ran a Sacramento store with his two sons, David and Moses (pictured here) until 1881, when the family moved to Los Angeles and established the famous Hamburger's Department Store.

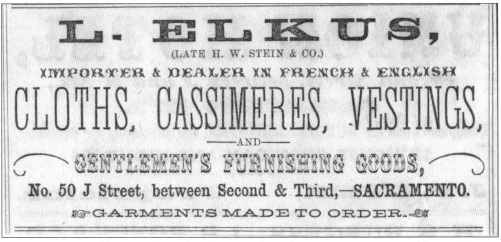

At age 12, Louis Elkus immigrated to America from the Prussian province of Posen. He was a well-known manufacturer and wholesale dealer in men's furnishing in San Francisco before relocating to Sacramento, where he served two terms as a county supervisor. Albert Elkus, the seventh of Louis's eight children, was born in Sacramento in 1857. He became a leading clothing merchant and political figure in the county.

Born in Bavaria in 1862, optometrist Siegfried G. Marshutz arrived in America in 1883. He established an optometric office in Sacramento. By 1885, he had moved to Los Angeles, where he formed another optometric group and was president of Congregation B'nai B'rith (today's Wilshire Boulevard Temple) and a founder of the Federation of Jewish Charities. Marshutz also served on the Los Angeles Library Commission from 1905 to 1908 before resigning to assume the presidency of the Jewish Orphans' Home, which was dedicated on January 31, 1909. He explained the need for the home in an article published in the *B'nai B'rith Messenger*: "Many [who come to Los Angeles for the healing climate] are so destitute that they cannot rear their children, others who do not find the desired relief in our climate, leave behind them widows and orphans. What, then, is the question, becomes of the little ones?" Siegfried Marshutz is pictured here at center, surrounded by colleagues.

The Sacramento store of Solomon Wasserman and Mark Davis, called the Nonpareil (having no equal), was located at the northeast corner of J and Fifth Streets. The dry and fancy goods store, pictured here in 1894, began three years earlier as the successor to S. Lipman & Co., which had been a Sacramento fixture for 25 years. Solomon Lipman was a charter member of Etham Lodge No. 37 of B'nai B'rith (established in 1858). Business at the Nonpareil was regular, with crowds of customers filling the store throughout the year. Solomon Wasserman and Mark Davis were considered experts in all details of the trade, as well as attentive and honest salesmen, and Wasserman was an officer of Congregation B'nai Israel. David Wasserman, Solomon's son, carried on the Nonpareil Department Store at 618 K Street with his business partner Julius S. Gattmann.

Bernard Ulmer Steinman left Germany for San Francisco at age 11, joining his older brother John, who operated a hotel. In the 1860s, Bernard moved to Sacramento, where he later served two terms as a county supervisor (1883–1891) and a term as mayor (1892–1896). He was also elected president of the Sacramento Gas and Electric Company in 1891 and became the founding president of the Farmers and Mechanics Bank in 1892.

Moses S. Wharhaftig fled oppressive conditions in Russia in 1882. He made his way to California, first working as a printer in San Francisco before taking up farming in Kings County near the town of Coalinga. Wharhaftig left the ranch in 1891 to settle in Sacramento, where he was eventually licensed to practice law. His fluency in Russian, Italian, and French made him an asset to Sacramento's judges, who often called on him as a translator.

Peter Wahrhaftig, Moses's brother, arrived in California in 1890 with his mother Rebecca, wife Leah, and their young sons. They initially joined Moses on the Kings County farm, but its isolation was not ideal for raising a family. Leah and Peter are seen here around 1920.

After about a year on the Kings County farm, Peter Wahrhaftig learned of a Russian Jewish farming colony in Orangevale, near Sacramento. The colony was formed by David Lubin and his half brother Harris Weinstock, who had settled 10 families on their fruit ranch. Wahrhaftig, pictured here with his four sons, moved his family to the colony.

During the 1890s, the Wahrhaftig family was centered in and around Sacramento. This photograph from around 1898 shows (seated, from left to right) Leah, Rebecca, and Peter; (standing in the back) Moses; and the four sons of Peter and Leah: Meyer, Solomon, Joseph, and Matt.

Matt Wahrhaftig, the youngest son of Peter and Leah, had a distinguished legal career in Oakland. After graduating from the University of California law school in 1914, he taught a number of courses at the school and started a successful law practice. He was counsel for such firms as the Alameda County Title Company, Farmers and Merchants Bank, and Crocker Bank.

David Lubin partnered with his half brother Harris Weinstock in a clothing business that grew into a department store, Weinstock, Lubin & Co., in 1874. The store occupied an imposing building on Sacramento's K Street. The business expanded into the Weinstock's department store chain (later purchased by Macy's). Lubin and Weinstock purchased land that became the Orangevale Jewish farming colony, located 15 miles east of Sacramento. Ten Russian Jewish families were settled on the land, which was irrigated by a water company the partners operated in Orangevale (originally for mining operations). The colony failed after about six years. San Francisco's *Emanu-El* newspaper reported on May 21, 1897, "Our limited efforts at colonization have been egregious failures . . . monuments of our benevolent folly or our foolish benevolence." Some blamed the colony's collapse on children who grew up and moved away without new settlers to replace them.

A native of central Poland, David Lubin arrived in the United States in the mid-1850s. After trying his hand in different places as a jeweler, lumberyard worker, gold prospector, and dry goods proprietor, he eventually opened the One-Price Store in Sacramento. The business grew into Weinstock, Lubin & Co. In 1884, after visiting agricultural settlements in Palestine, Lubin was convinced that the future of the world depended on the cultivation of soil. He helped found the California Fruit Growers' Union and directed the International Society for the Colonization of Russian Jews. Together with his son Simon, he wrote a proposal for an international chamber of agriculture. He moved to Italy in 1896, and his International Institute of Agriculture opened in Rome in 1905 with the support of Italy's King Victor Emmanuel. David Lubin was the institute's American delegate until his death in Rome in 1919 at age 69.

Born in London to Polish immigrant parents, Harris Weinstock took an active role in Sacramento's civic and Jewish affairs. He served as president of Congregation B'nai Israel, brought in Rabbi Joseph Leonard Levy from England to lead the congregation, and lectured widely on Jews in American life. In 1913, Pres. Woodrow Wilson appointed Weinstock to the Commission on Industrial Relations.

The impressive Sacramento home of Harris Weinstock reflected his stature in the community. In addition to his business and Jewish involvements, he was the first president of the Commonwealth Club of San Francisco, a member of the California State Board of Horticulture, and a labor relations expert.

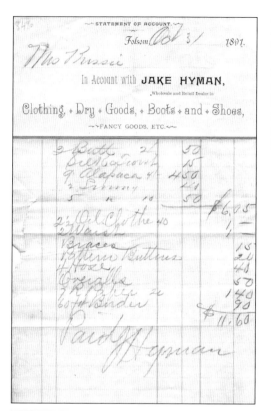

Jacob Hyman started a dry goods business in Folsom with Solomon Zekind in 1865. When the partnership dissolved a year later, the *Folsom Telegraph* reported that Hyman was setting out on his own: "Mr. Hyman is well known to our citizens and has built up for himself a large and thriving business and always maintained the reputation of a fair and honest merchant. Give him a call."

Polish-born Edward Levy settled in Folsom in the 1860s and opened a wholesale and retail liquor and tobacco store on Sutter Street. This store ledger from the 1910s lists the address as "Levy's Building," an indication of the size and prominence to which his business had grown.

Much of Edward Levy's success owed to his professional demeanor and interpersonal skills. His fluency in German and Yiddish was an asset during the Gold Rush days, when many of the new arrivals struggled with language barriers. In 1873, Levy purchased a house on the northeast corner of Scott and Figueroa Streets. The house remained in the family for nearly a century. Although not particularly observant, Levy and his family attended High Holiday services in Sacramento and forbade pork products in the house. However, he regularly received oysters packed in ice from Eugene Levy of San Francisco, who may have been a brother or cousin. In 1926, Folsom's Masonic Lodge presented Levy with a certificate honoring him for serving more than 50 years as treasurer of the lodge. He died the following year at age 88.

Polish native Augusta Golde had known Edward Levy in Europe before he left for America. The two reconnected in Sacramento, where they were married on October 5, 1869, at the home of Joseph Fiel. Augusta and Edward had three daughters: Hattie, Irma Ruth, and Lotta. All three graduated from high school in Folsom.

Hattie Levy became Folsom's first public librarian when a branch of the Sacramento County Library opened in 1906 (pictured here). She was married to Ward Morrison of Boston, a non-Jew. Their son Edward Levy Morrison entered the University of California in Berkeley in 1920, at which time Hattie transferred to an Oakland library. Her sister Lotta took over as Folsom's librarian until her death in 1955.

Born in New York in 1851, Philip C. Cohn arrived in Folsom in the 1880s and established a mercantile business. A major landowner, Cohn acquired farms in the Orangevale district and El Dorado County, seven acres on the shore of Lake Tahoe, and city properties in San Francisco, Sacramento, Folsom, and elsewhere. He was a member of numerous fraternal organizations, including B'nai B'rith, director of the Consumers' Ice and Cold Storage Company, and an organizer and board member of the Capital Fire Insurance Company of Sacramento. His eclectic mansion at 305 Scott Street in Folsom was built in the early 1890s. It is one of three Victorian homes on Nob Hill overlooking Old Folsom's Sutter Street Mall. Philip Cohn designed the house himself, and it remained in the Cohn family for over 70 years.

In

Memory of

SOPHIA EISNER.

Who departed this Life

April 5th 1862,

Aged

4 months & 5 days.

Folsom's old Jewish Cemetery, now at the western edge of Lakeside Memorial Lawn Cemetery, was established in 1861 by the Hebrew Benevolent Society, an organization founded in 1860 at the urging of a traveler named I.J. Benjamin. The cemetery's first burial was that of infant Sophia Eisner. The site has 36 existing headstones, along with a dozen or so burials without headstones. The only family plot remaining belongs to Jacob Hyman, who is buried alongside his wife, Belle, and their son Isaac. Descendants of the Cohn, Hyman, and Jacobs families were trustees of the cemetery before portions of the property were deeded to the Masons. The remainder went to Lee Miller around 1958, who promised that the Jewish burial sites would be preserved and maintained.

Simon Cohn was the father-in-law of Phillip Cohn. (The two happened to share the same last name.) Born in Poland in 1830, Simon arrived in California via the Nicaragua route and, after experiencing ups and downs in San Francisco, opened Cohn's General Merchant Store in Folsom in 1856. Part of the Cohn mansion on Nob Hill comprises Simon's house, which was connected to the larger structure by a short passageway.

Abraham Cohn, a younger relative of Simon Cohn and a native of Poland, is also interred in the Jewish section of Folsom's Lakeside Memorial Lawn Cemetery. He became a member of the Mutual Hook and Ladder Company, joining fellow Jewish merchants Joseph Fiel and Jacob Hyman, among others.

Jacob Hyman, a native of Germany, sailed to the United States around 1851 and made his way to California in 1854. He became one of Folsom's leading dry goods merchants. At one time, his baroque Victorian mansion, built in 1881 and still standing at 603 Figueroa on Nob Hill above Sutter Street, had a fireplace in nearly every room. He also built the Hyman building at Sutter and Wool Streets. Jacob and Belle Hyman had two daughters, Rose and Laura, and two sons, Isaac and Walter. Walter, pictured here with his wife and daughter, struck gold as a young man and kept a room at San Francisco's Palace Hotel until his money ran out. He also strung the first powerlines in Folsom. Years later, the company was sold to Pacific Gas and Electric.

*Seven*

# SAN JOAQUIN COUNTY

Between 1843 and 1846, when California was a province of independent Mexico, five land grants were made in what would later become San Joaquin County, named for the San Joaquin River, which springs from the southern Sierra Nevada. Weber Point, in the county seat of Stockton, had the first permanent residence in the San Joaquin Valley. The home belonged to Capt. Charles Weber, a German immigrant who briefly tried gold mining before realizing that supplying miners was much more profitable. Captain Weber founded Stockton in 1849 after purchasing 49,000 acres. Stockton had various names in the early years, including Tuleburg and Mudville, but Weber decided on Stockton to honor Commodore Robert F. Stockton, who was instrumental in the capture of California during the Mexican-American War (1846–1848). This made Stockton the first California community with an English name, rather than one derived from Spanish or a Native American language. An important inland port during the Gold Rush years, Stockton was transformed from a small settlement to a major commercial center. Area merchants supplied miners on their way to the Sierra foothills. Jewish immigrants took advantage of these conditions, establishing a thriving community in the early 1850s.

Ryhim Ahoovim (Beloved Friends) was formed in 1851 as Stockton's Hebrew Benevolent Society and formally organized as a Polish Orthodox congregation in 1855. Capt. Charles M. Weber, the founder of Stockton, donated a parcel of land to Ryhim Ahoovim on the north bank of the Stockton Channel, near Miner and Hunter Streets. There were no sawmills in the area, so lumber had to be shipped around Cape Horn, unloaded at the Stockton waterfront, and hauled to the building site by congregants. The building was completed and dedicated on August 28, 1855, just four months after the congregation was formed. Inaugural services were conducted by Rabbi Julius Eckman of San Francisco. The synagogue eventually became known as Temple Israel, one of the state's three oldest Jewish congregations.

When Solomon Friedlander, a young merchant from Poland, passed away on October 4, 1851, members of Rhyim Ahoovim met to discuss the creation of a Jewish cemetery. Once again, they turned to Charles M. Weber, who generously donated a 300-foot-square block bounded by North Union, East Poplar, North Pilgrim, and East Acacia Streets, on the edge of the growing city. The site became known as Temple Israel Cemetery.

Shortly after its founding in 1851, a fence was built around the perimeter of Temple Israel Cemetery. The site became a California Registered Historical Landmark on December 10, 1961. A plaque adjacent to the entrance reads, "It is the oldest Jewish cemetery in continuous use in California and west of the Rocky Mountains."

TILLIE EHRLICH LEWIS

JULY 13, 1901

APRIL 30, 1977

הנצב״ה

Temple Israel Cemetery remains active to the present day. Among the notable people buried there is Tillie Lewis, America's first female captain of industry. Lewis established major agricultural canning plants in San Joaquin and Stanislaus Counties. During the Great Depression, she invited people of all backgrounds, regardless of race, gender, or religion, into her workforce. By 1950, her company grew into the fifth largest canning business in the United States. She was named Businesswoman of the Year by the Associated Press in 1951. The following year, she launched the Tasti-Diet, the first diet and diet products approved by the American Medical Association. Her husband, labor organizer Meyer Lewis, is interred next to her. The couple met in 1940, when Meyer helped Tillie negotiate a contract with her employees. They were married seven years later.

Herman Davidson, born Zvi Herschel Kantorowitz in Russia, served Ryhim Ahoovim as rabbi and cantor during the late 19th century. Although he was an opera singer without formal rabbinic training, Davidson had a strong Orthodox background that fit the congregation's original designation as an Orthodox synagogue. In 1897, he married Carrie Snow, the daughter of Placerville pioneer Samuel Sussman Snow.

Other members of the Kantorowitz family also made the journey from Russia to Stockton. Sadie Kantorowitz, the sister of Herman Davidson, married Max Sinai in Russia. He first traveled alone to Stockton, and was later joined by Sadie and their children in 1891. Fannie Sinai, the daughter of Max and Sadie, is pictured here.

Ryhim Ahoovim officially became a Reform congregation in 1892. Even before that time, services had included some nontraditional elements, such as a pipe organ, mixed choir, and mixed seating. By the early 1890s, membership had dropped to only 19. To attract more interest, the congregation adopted the modernizing outlook of Reform Judaism. Rabbi-Cantor Herman Davidson was dismissed in 1896 to make room for a Reform rabbi. The controversial decision was reported on the front page of the *Stockton Mail* on October 26, 1896. The rabbinic post was empty until August 1, 1898, when the congregation hired Rabbi Rudolph Farber, who had previously served in San Francisco. Herman Davidson returned briefly to be the cantor, but when traditionalist members left to form two new synagogues, Davidson was made leader of one of them, Ahavas Achim (Brotherly Love).

Ray Frank, a native of San Francisco, was the first Jewish woman to formally preach in the United States. Although not technically a rabbi, a male-only profession at the time, Frank was known as the "Girl Rabbi of the Golden West." She spent much of the 1890s leading Jewish services and speaking at West Coast synagogues, B'nai B'rith lodges, literary societies, and women's groups.

In April 1897, Ray Frank was invited to conduct Passover services at Stockton's Ryhim Ahoovim. Tensions had flared between the congregation's Reform and Orthodox members, and Frank was called upon to help restore the peace. Her efforts were successful, but when the congregation's president reportedly wanted to hire her as rabbi, protests erupted among conservative members.

In 1900, Ryhim Ahoovim, now known as Temple Israel, established a fund for a new building on Hunter Street. The synagogue was completed and dedicated in 1904, coinciding with the congregation's 50th anniversary. Temple Israel joined the Reform movement's Union of American Hebrew Congregations in 1906. The architecture was in keeping with the Reform aesthetic of the time. However, even with the attractive new building, the congregation struggled to retain a rabbi. Of the nine who served there between 1901 and 1929, only two, Louis J. Kopald and Emmanuel Jack, stayed for more than three years (they lasted four years each). In 1924, Temple Israel received a puzzling letter and donation from the local chapter of the Ku Klux Klan, Stockton Klan No. 3. The letter read in part: "While we are a White, Gentile, Protestant Organization, we are always glad to be of some service to our Brothers of the Jewish Faith."

Aaron L. Sapiro is pictured to the left of Rabbi Louis J. Kopald, who served Temple Israel of Stockton from 1909 to 1913. Sapiro was a teacher at the temple's religious school when this photograph was taken. One of seven children of Polish Jewish immigrants, he became a prominent attorney specializing in farming cooperatives. In 1925, he filed a libel suit in Detroit's federal court against Henry Ford, who had published anti-Semitic accusations against him in the *Dearborn Independent*. Opponents of organized farming disseminated the articles to farmers, stoking fears that Jews were trying to control and exploit them. Following a mistrial, the suit was set to return to court in the summer of 1927. Before the trial got underway, Ford ended his long campaign against the Jews and agreed to Sapiro's demands: a personal apology, payment of his legal fees, and a full retraction of his newspaper's anti-Jewish accusations.

San Francisco native Edgar F. Magnin served Temple Israel as a student rabbi during the 1913 High Holiday services. He returned after his ordination in 1914, but only stayed until the end of 1915. During his installation service, Magnin announced his intention to deliver a series of Friday night sermons. The first sermon, "Idols, Old and New," would deal with the apathy many Jews felt toward Judaism. While serving in Stockton, he visited Fresno to organize that city's Temple Beth Israel. David Greenberg, who served as Temple Israel's student rabbi in 1926, was elected rabbi of the Fresno synagogue in 1931 and remained there until his retirement 40 years later. Magnin moved on to Congregation B'nai B'rith of Los Angeles, today's Wilshire Boulevard Temple, where he served for 69 years until his death in 1984.

120

Stockton and its Jewish community grew considerably after World War II. The period brought stability to Temple Israel, which had a long history of rabbis with very short tenures. Rabbi Bernard Rosenberg came to Stockton in 1956 and remained for 21 years. He was well regarded in the city, combining rabbinical duties with civic engagement. Rosenberg also lectured in Judaic studies at the University of the Pacific, a private university in Stockton. In 1960, Temple Israel purchased three acres at El Dorado Street and March Lane from Captain Weber's grandson. The new structure, designed to accommodate the growing membership, was built slowly, with classrooms and offices being erected first. The temple's third (and current) sanctuary was finally completed and dedicated in 1972. A monument representing the Ten Commandments stands outside the synagogue.

Jacob Glick established a successful jewelry store in Stockton in 1876. Later called Glick Jewelers, the business remained in the family for over a century. Glick served as an officer of Temple Israel, and was present at the installation ceremony for Rabbi Edgar Magnin in 1914.

A native of Germany, Solomon Sweet arrived in San Francisco in 1850. He worked for a time in Stockton before moving to Agua Fria, a mining town at the northern edge of the San Joaquin Valley. He operated a store there until 1857, when he settled in Visalia in the lower San Joaquin Valley. Sweet opened the mercantile firm of S. Sweet & Co. with his brother Simon.

Morris Weinstein operated a men's clothing store on Stockton's Weber Avenue from 1900 to 1920. A native of Russia, Weinstein lived on the East Coast and in Honolulu, Hawaii, before settling in California. He spoke fluent Spanish and recruited Mexican laborers for an Alaskan fish-packing firm.

This photograph of Stockton's public bathhouse, taken around 1900, features an advertisement for the IXL clothing store written in the style of Brother Jonathan, a popular humorist of the period. Located at Main and El Dorado Streets, IXL was owned by Max Goldsmith and Joseph Steinhart and specialized in men's clothing and shoes.

A brass plaque on the sidewalk at the northeast corner of Main and American Streets honors A.B. Cohn, founder of the Stockton Dry Goods Co. The plaque was laid in 1935 to commemorate the store's 21st anniversary.

Lena Levinsky Bruml, a native of Prussia, married Moses Bruml in Sacramento in 1857. They resided in Jackson until 1869, when they relocated to Lockeford. The Brumls had four children, all born in Jackson: Albert, Amelia, Julius, and Henry. Lena was also the great-aunt of Alice B. Toklas.

Moses Bruml, a trained cobbler and Bohemian native, applied his trade in Budapest, Hungary, for a number of years. He arrived in California in 1852, working for a year as a peddler and clerk in Sacramento before relocating to Jackson, where he opened a bar and variety store. While in Jackson, Bruml was active at Stockton's Temple Israel. In 1869, he purchased a general merchandise store from his brother-in-law Louis Levinsky in Lockeford, a small town in San Joaquin County. M. Bruml General Merchandise stocked groceries, provisions, dry goods, boots, shoes, hardware, drugs, wines, liquors, and cigars. Moses Bruml's son Julius later joined the firm, and the name was changed to Bruml & Son. After Moses died in 1901, the firm was run by Julius and his brother Henry as Bruml Bros. The family kept the Lockeford store for three decades, during which time they were the only Jews in the vicinity.

# BIBLIOGRAPHY

Aron, Stephen. *The American West: A Very Short Introduction*. New York, NY: Oxford University Press, 2015.

Epstein, David W. *Why the Jews Were So Successful in the Wild West and How to Tell Their Stories*. Woodland Hills, CA: Isaac Nathan, 2007.

Epstein, David W., and Regina Merwin. "Western States Jewish History 40-Year Person Index." *Western States Jewish History* 40:3/4 (2008): 349–423.

Friedmann, Jonathan L. *Jews, Music and the American West: Portraits of Pioneers*. Santa Fe, NM: Gaon, 2016.

Morris, Susan. *A Traveler's Guide to Pioneer Jewish Cemeteries of the California Gold Rush*. Berkeley, CA: Judah L. Magnes Museum, 1996.

Rischin, Moses, and John Livingston, ed. *Jews of the American West*. Detroit, MI: Wayne State University Press, 1991.

Rochlin, Harriet, and Fred Rochlin. *Pioneer Jews: A New Life in the Far West*. New York, NY: Mariner, 2000.

Starr, Kevin. *California: A History*. New York, NY: Modern Library, 2005.

Sturman, Gladys, and David Epstein. "Postscript: The Western States Jewish History Archives." *A Cultural History of Jews in California*. Bruce Zuckerman, William Deverell, and Lisa Ansell, eds. 47–54. West Lafayette, IN: Purdue University Press, 2009.

Szasz, Ferenc Morton. *Religion in the Modern American West*. Tucson, AZ: University of Arizona Press, 2000.

Walsh, Margaret. *The American West: Visions and Revisions*. New York, NY: Cambridge University Press, 2005.

# ABOUT THE ORGANIZATION

Established in 1968, the Western States Jewish History Association (WSJHA) is dedicated to the discovery, collection, and dissemination of items and information pertaining to Jews of the region. The online Jewish Museum of the American West, a subsidiary of WSJHA, features hundreds of exhibits on the region's early Jewish pioneers.

# DISCOVER THOUSANDS OF LOCAL HISTORY BOOKS FEATURING MILLIONS OF VINTAGE IMAGES

Arcadia Publishing, the leading local history publisher in the United States, is committed to making history accessible and meaningful through publishing books that celebrate and preserve the heritage of America's people and places.

## Find more books like this at
## www.arcadiapublishing.com

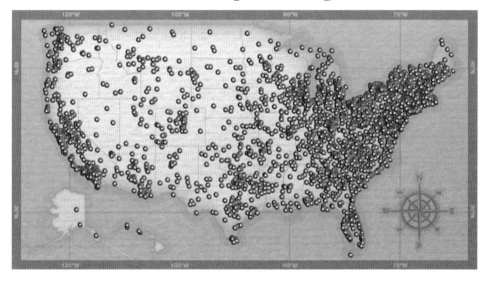

Search for your hometown history, your old stomping grounds, and even your favorite sports team.

Consistent with our mission to preserve history on a local level, this book was printed in South Carolina on American-made paper and manufactured entirely in the United States. Products carrying the accredited Forest Stewardship Council (FSC) label are printed on 100 percent FSC-certified paper.

MADE IN THE USA